# ORACLE BONES
# DIVINATION

# ORACLE BONES DIVINATION

## THE GREEK I CHING

### KOSTAS DERVENIS

Destiny Books
Rochester, Vermont • Toronto, Canada

Destiny Books
One Park Street
Rochester, Vermont 05767
www.DestinyBooks.com

Destiny Books is a division of Inner Traditions International

Originally published in Greek under the title *Manteia ton Astragalon* [Divination
   by astragalomancy] by Esoptron Publications
First U.S. edition published in 2014 by Destiny Books

**Library of Congress Cataloging-in-Publication Data**
Dervenis, Kostas.
  [Manteia ton astragalon. English]
  Oracle bones divination : the Greek I ching / Kostas Dervenis.
    pages cm
  Includes bibliographical references.
  Summary: "The first complete guide to this ancient Greek form of divination" —
Provided by publisher.
  ISBN 978-1-62055-101-1 (pbk.) — ISBN 978-1-62055-164-6 (e-book)
  1. Scapulimancy—Greece. 2. Oracle bones—Greece. 3. Divination—Greece. 4.
Oracles, Greek.  I. Title. II. Title: Greek I ching.
  BF1779.S32D47155 2014
  133.3—dc23
                                                         2013021695
Printed and bound in Canada by Marquis

10 9 8 7 6 5 4 3 2 1

Text design and layout by Brian Boynton
This book was typeset in Garamond Premier Pro with Gill Sans and Caxton as
display typefaces

To send correspondence to the author of this book, mail a first-class letter to the
author c/o Inner Traditions • Bear & Company, One Park Street, Rochester, VT
05767, and we will forward the communication.

# CONTENTS

# FOREWORD

## Resurrecting a Lost Tradition

In ancient Greece, as in most places where archaic cultures once thrived, methods of foretelling the future—whether they were "official" oracles of the gods or simply people tossing a pair of dice for luck—were widespread. These customs stopped being publicly practiced due to incessant pressure from the Greek Orthodox Church, following the establishment of Christianity as a state religion. The church viewed divination as a forbidden pagan practice that had to be removed from public life at all cost. Despite centuries of persecution, however, most of Greece's ancient traditions survived to the modern era relatively unscathed by taking refuge in the cradle of "folk belief." Hence, formerly religious practices such as hydromancy (divination using water), pyromancy (divination using fire), augury (divination by omens), and astragalomancy itself (divination using sheep bones as ritual dice) were handed down from father to son and mother to daughter, in existence in almost every remote town and village in Greece. Many well-known folklorists have made reference to these traditions in their works.

From that perspective, the real value of this book lies not only in the fact that it is the first presentation of Greek astragalomancy in the past century, providing a place for the art next to the Taoist I Ching and Western tarot. Its value lies not only in the fact that it offers an official record of a forgotten method of divination (which, as we have stated repeatedly, is still widespread throughout Greece in the form of games of chance using sheep bones). No, the real value of this book lies in that, for the first time since it was lost millennia ago, the author has reconstructed the complete matrix of a complex ancient system of divination, using original stanzas discovered in ancient Greek temples and formerly lost to time.

Hence this book should in no way be compared to the many other volumes flooding the market that proclaim they can foretell the future using unproven or nonexistent methods. The wisdom and functionality that differentiate this particular volume characterize it not only as an important point of inspiration and guidance for its user, but as a precious jewel resurrecting an authentic ancient Greek tradition.

STAMOS STINIS, PUBLISHER,
*ESOPTRON PUBLICATIONS*
ATHENS, GREECE

# PROLOGUE

This book explores the ancient practice of *astragalomancy*, which uses the anklebones of an animal (*astragali*, plural, or *astragalus*, singular) as ritual tools within a system of divination. The text of the divinations found in part 2 of this book originates, for the most part, from Greek temples in Asia Minor. Specifically, the verses are from ancient Greek temples in modern Turkey: at Kosagatch (ancient Lycia), at Tefeny and Yarishli (ancient Phrygia), at Enevre (Anaboura), at Sagalassos and Termessos (ancient Pisidia), at Attalia (ancient Pamphylia), and at Ördekj and Indjik.

Since 1912, it has been generally accepted that these verses, discovered in the ruins of the temples at the aforementioned sites, constitute fragments of a single encoded method of astragalomancy, a method that has been lost to us (or perhaps not yet fully uncovered by the archaeologist's pick). Unfortunately, the verses have not survived in their complete form, but only as fragments. It was up to us, then, but mostly up to our sources (the researchers of the nineteenth and early twentieth centuries who discovered the original artifacts), to complete the text found in the remains. The publications used to reconstruct the text are included in the bibliography.

I am grateful for the assistance of Spyridoula Klabatsea in the translation of these verses. For some verses we relied exclusively on the derivations and interpretations provided by our sources. For others, we disagreed with our sources partially or totally, and so edited and completed the text as we thought best. As a consequence, the presentation and format of the divinations should be viewed as our exclusive responsibility—our interpretation of the archaeological record. All credit should go to our sources, while the blame for any errors discovered lies unquestionably with the author.

PART I

# *Introduction to Divination*
## Determining One's Fate and Fortune

From the depths of far distant time, people have feared for their future. Our hopes and worries for the morrow have held us in thrall since organized societies were first developed, and with them the concept of ownership. Individuals as well as whole nations have, from the most ancient of days, expressed this basic need for foreknowledge of their fate in war, in peace, in commerce, and in love. Divination was the means by which a person, or a society, could learn the will of the gods and ask them for guidance.

# HOW THE ANCIENT GREEKS VIEWED FATE

Why did all ancient peoples—and the Greeks in particular—rely on divination? Was it simply, as stated, the fear for tomorrow that has plagued humankind since the beginning? Or was it that they viewed Fate as *not* predetermined and static, but rather as a tendency, a flowing pattern that could be changed? Perhaps divination was, in the end, a sort of prayer, a plea to divine authority that we may circumvent the negative and seek the positive. "All things are in flux," as Heraclitus boldly declared so long ago—the universe manifests itself as a series of possibilities, and circumstances do not take shape until the events and decisions that precede them are finalized. This typology, which corresponds so well with the theories of modern physics, is quite apparent in the deified version of the Fates in ancient Greece.

The Fates, called Moirai ("Those who Divide and Assign"), were three: Lachesis ("She Who Draws Lots"), Clotho ("The Spinner"), and Atropos ("She Who May Not Be Turned"). With their mother, Ananke ("Need/Necessity/Desire"), they determine the destiny of the universe.

Ananke emerged self-formed at the very beginning of time, according to Plato—an incorporeal being encompassing the breadth and width of the universe. From the first moment, Ananke was entwined with the serpentine coils of her mate, Cronos, or Time. Together they

*Ananke on high with the three Fates below her*

brought about the formation of the ordered universe, the encircling forces of Necessity and Time, impelling the motion of the heavens. Ananke is characterized both by her omniscience and the capability to alter destiny by virtue of her essence, without requisite action. In Platonic theory, it is thought that the great Tapestry of the Universe rests on her knees.* In many respects, the form of Ananke is reminiscent of the Buddhist concept of *karma.* Of Necessity, then, were borne the three Fates.

---

*Proclus, *On the Theology of Plato,* book 6.

The Fates were subject to hierarchy. "The Moirai, daughters of Ananke, clad in white vestments. . . . Lachesis, Clotho, and Atropos, who sing in unison. . . . Lachesis singing of things that were, Clotho the things that are, and Atropos of things that are to be," writes Plato in the *Republic*. According to the Neo-Platonist philosopher Proclus, this symbolism outlines their relationship: the past was once the present and the future, while the present was once the future. Hence, Lachesis contains Clotho and Atropos, while Clotho contains only Atropos. The three Fates partially embrace and partially abstain from the world. They turn the Heavenly Spheres, Lachesis with both hands, Clotho with her right, and Atropos with her left—another indication of their hierarchy.

When a soul is brought into the world by its allotted deity, it first submits to Lachesis, then to Clotho and then to Atropos. Finally, it kneels before the throne of Ananke and is subsequently brought to the field of Oblivion and the River Forgetfulness. Oblivion and Forgetfulness make the soul suffer while it is in the world, given that, because of them, it cannot comprehend that its suffering is due to Universal Necessity. When a soul discovers its own esoteric godhood, however, and the "Internal Acropolis" arises from within, then it can face its Destiny without fear and boldly testify, "I surrender myself to Clotho."* When using the oracle bones, we entreat Clotho to weave a more positive thread into our own personal pattern, before her younger sister Atropos finalizes our destiny with her shears.†

---

*Marcus Aurelius, *The Meditations*.

†Interestingly enough, the earliest known text referring to the Fates is a papyrus fragment discovered in 1962 in the Derveni pass in northern Greece, known as the Derveni Papyrus. I would like to think that this synonymy is Clotho's work, as it appears that the Lady has a well-developed sense of humor.

# THE HISTORY OF
# THE ORACLE BONES
# (ASTRAGALI)

Divination played a major role in the ancient Greek religion. The philosopher Plato in *Phaedrus* distinguishes two major categories of divination. The first type is immediate and is called *intuitive* divination: it is based on contact between a gifted individual and a god or spirit. The seeress Pythia of Delphi, for instance, was an example of divinely inspired intuitive divination. The second category is indirect and refers to *inferential* or *interpretive* divination. This type of divination does not require the wielder to have any specific gift but is undertaken through a ritualistic methodology whose intent is the interpretation of divine will, a method that may be taught and passed on from individual to individual.

Ancient writers recorded fifty-eight types of divination practiced by the ancient Greeks. Cleromancy, or divination by lots, was one of them. In particular, cleromancy through the use of astragalus bones was very popular. The astragali were anklebones from the rear hooves of different animals, mostly sheep, goats, deer, and ox. They were essentially used in a fashion similar to dice and are commonly known today by their English names "knucklebones" or "hucklebones."

*Astragalus bones*

Games of chance played with astragali were common in ancient Greece—indeed, they are still played today in rural areas of modern Greece—and were popular among both children and adults. The early development of astragalus games, however, is tied to divination, and has its roots in Neolithic times or earlier. Astragalus bones most likely used for divination were found in the Neolithic village of Çatal Höyuk in Anatolia in Asia Minor, dating to the sixth millenniumBCE. In addition, a golden astragalus dated to the fifth millennium BCE was found in Bulgaria. It seems that divination using astragalus bones represents a ritual widespread throughout the entire eastern Mediterranean, a ritual that eventually degraded into a game of chance in classical Greece and Rome. Astragali have been used, and continue to be used, for gaming from the Atlantic to the Ural Mountains, and from the Americas to Mongolia. In ancient Rome a popular board game played using astragalus bones was known as *tali*. In Greece astragalus bones were used as dice in a number of early games: *astragalismos, artiasmos, pentalitha* ("five stones," still played in parts of the world today), *omilla,* and others. The popularity of these games reached its peak in Greece and Asia Minor during the classical period.

*Roman girl playing astragalus*

To honor the sanctity of the astragali, and to make them easier to use, the ancients fabricated imitations from various materials: bronze, copper, clay, enamel, ivory, agate, marble, lead, semiprecious stones, silver, and gold. They produced special containers, some tastefully made and others not, for those astragali that had a higher monetary value. In addition, in many children's graves archaeologists have found a sack of astragali in the left hand of the remains, testament not only of the parents' love for their child and of their desire to send his favorite toys with him on to the next life, but also of the inviolability of astragali in general and their origin in primal sacrament.

*Special astragalus containers*

Sophocles attributes the invention of astragali to Palamedes, who taught the Greeks how to play the game (as a game rather than a method of divination) during the Trojan War. Plato and Herodotus disagree with him. Plato in *Phaedrus* attributes the discovery of astragali to the Egyptian god Thoth, whom many consider to be equivalent to Hermes. Herodotus attributes the development of the game to the Lydians of Asia Minor. Plato's opinion coincides with that of many modern scholars, who consider the spread of astragali to be tied to the worship of Hermes, or to the worship of the three Fates in earlier times. Perhaps Hermes was a far more important figure in the eastern Mediterranean in archaic times than the simple messenger of the gods he became during the classical period. In any case, as the worship of the God of the Sun Apollo grew more important than the worship of the Fates or Hermes—and more important than the other chthonic gods of the Earth that were venerated with them—divination with astragalus bones became the prerogative of Apollo. Today, most of the verses that have been uncovered refer to him as the tutelary deity.

*Statue of the Sun God Apollo*

More than twenty-two thousand astragali were uncovered in the Korykeion Cave at Delphi, offerings to Apollo. In fact, Apollo became, during classical times, the de facto god of divination, and it is to him that most temples serving as oracles were offered. The most famous of these is, of course, Delphi, which played a major role in the political, private, and public lives of the Greeks. But Delphi was not the only oracle of Apollo. On continental Greece, there were Apollonian oracles in Aves of Fokis prefecture; at Thebes, Tegyra, and Ptoos of Boeotia prefecture; and at Koropi in Thessalia prefecture. There was an oracle dedicated to Apollo Deiradiotis in Argos, while a "branch office" of the Delphic Oracle operated in Gortyna on the island of Crete. In

*Temple of Apollo, Delphi*

Lesbos we find the oracle of Apollo Napaios, while in Delos there is an Apollonian oracle on the peak of Mount Kynthos. For the purposes of this text, it is important to note that Apollo's fame as an oracle had spread to neighboring Ionia and Lycia in Asia Minor. There were Apollonian oracles at Gryneio, Didyma, Claro, and Patara.

In broader terms, then, divination through the use of animal bones in general, and anklebones in particular, is a primal and universal practice that has its roots in Paleolithic times. We can even state that it continues to be practiced around the world today in both its original and modified forms. The celebrated Chinese I Ching, which has been dated to 1000 BCE, was initially based on the interpretation of cracks on the shells of tortoises, following their ritualistic burning. The I Ching is simply one more variety of bone oracle. The Chinese, being a practical people, sought more efficient means of generating the binary code necessary to their oracle, and discovered this means in the use of yarrow stalks, which eventually evolved into the popular coin method.

The final version of the I Ching, which has been widely translated and is widely used today, was likely formulated in the second century BCE. Hence it would not be farfetched to say that divination through the use of astragali predates the I Ching by four thousand to five thousand years, making it the oldest form of cleromancy extant in the world today!

# HOW TO CAST
# THE ORACLE

Every astragalus bone has four sides, two of which are narrow and two broad. The broad convex side is called *pranes,* while the broad concave side is called *hyption.* The convex narrow side is called *chion,* while the concave narrow side is called *koon.* Hence, the possible outcomes of each throw are called *koon, chion, hyption,* and *pranes.* The koon throw is worth six points, while the chion throw is worth one. Of the two broad sides, the hyption throw receives three points, while the pranes four. The chion throw was also called *monos* (single), and the koon throw *exetis* (sixes), based on the numerical values they represented.

Γ, hyption    Δ, pranes    Ϲ, koon    Δ, chion

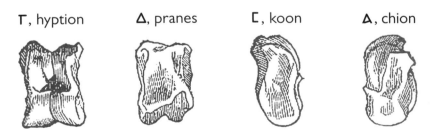

*The four potential tosses of an astragalus bone*

Before questioning the oracle, we must first clearly establish what it is that we would like to ask. The more specific and precise a question is, the clearer the answer that you receive will be.

While procuring, cleaning, and sanctifying sheep anklebones is the traditional method for using this oracle, it would be presumptuous to require the reader to indulge in such ritual.* Moreover, there is little time and inclination in modern day for such excesses. Thankfully, there is no need. To borrow from a Chinese method developed in centuries past for convenience's sake, we can also use coins with the astragali oracle. Take three coins that you will from that point on use only for this purpose. The value of these coins is not important; what is important is that you treat them with respect from then on. The variations in the values of the coins correlate to the four sides of an astragalus. When tossing the coins, their accumulative value is calculated as follows.

| Bone Position | Greek Position Name and Symbol | Coin Equivalent Configuration | Point Value |
|---|---|---|---|
| | chion, Λ | H H H | 1 |
| | hyption, Γ | T H H | 3 |
| | pranes, Δ | T T H | 4 |
| | koon, C | T T T | 6 |

*For those interested, the anklebones are boiled, scraped clean, then boiled once again in a very dilute solution of vinegar and water. They are then scraped clean again, allowed to soak, washed again, and so on until completely clean and free of flesh and blood.

## Casting the Oracle Coins

Sit where you feel most comfortable, ideally at a desk or at a table. Make sure the area in front of you is neat and clean.

On a piece of paper, or in a notebook dedicated for this purpose, write down the question that you would like to ask of the oracle.

Concentrate on the question, repeating it in your mind.

Relax. Take a deep inhalation down into the center of your belly, breathing as a baby breathes, and hold that inhalation briefly.

Toss the three coins.

Establish the numerical value that the faces of the coins stand for as described above.

Do this four more times, representing a total of five throws of a single astragalus or a single toss of five astragali. Make sure that you retain your concentration and briefly hold your breath each time you make a throw.

Add up the total. Refer to the "List of Divination Combinations" at the back of the book (page 163). Find the divination that correlates to the total numerical value you have thrown. There is an oracular verse corresponding to the precise configuration of each possible throw.

In most cases, the oracle will answer you directly without runaround or subtleties. In this light, the astragali are very different from the I Ching, which is often more tactful and somewhat evasive. Perhaps this comes down to a simple difference in Western and Eastern mindsets. In any case, it is up to you whether or not you want to follow the oracle's advice.

It may be prudent to mention a cultural and historic characteristic of the text in order to avoid provoking confusion. Many of the stanzas refer to the gods of ancient Greece. Readers will notice that a specific verse will call upon a given classical deity—and this is natural, because the original text predates Christian times by centuries. Of course, this does not mean that the reader has to follow the oracle's advice verbatim! When a given verse refers you to a select deity, in essence it is advising you to request divine aid, and it is best that you do this in accord with your own personal religious persuasion. In the same light, readers who are familiar with ancient Greek will notice that the text uses terminology that has differentiated in the modern day from its original meaning. Hence the word *theos* (god) simply means "powerful one" in ancient Greek and refers to the Divine, or to a tutelary spiritual entity such as a guardian angel. Similarly, the word *daemon* means "wise one," not "demon," and refers to the "powerful one" corresponding to each individual divination. It would be a mistake to regard this terminology in a Judeo-Christian context.

For those readers who would like to expand their understanding of the Greek gods mentioned in the divinations, refer to the next chapter, "The Greek Gods," which contains an alphabetical list of the gods and descriptions of their roles and abilities.

# THE GREEK GODS

For the ancient Greeks, the significance of the gods and supernatural beings in the divinations would have been self-explanatory. The Greeks cultivated a patronal system of gods and spirits who served specific human needs, conditions, or desires and to whom one would give praise or tribute for success in particular fields. Modern readers may have to take a more conscious approach to interpreting the divinations. As mentioned in the previous chapter, all divinations should be acted upon (or not acted upon) according to one's personal religious beliefs; however, additional context can certainly aid understanding. The following alphabetical list provides a taste of that context.

## ADRASTEIA

"She whom none can escape." Possibly an epithet of Rhea Cybele in her attribute as the Mother who punishes human injustice and upholds the natural order of the universe, the Greeks and Romans later identified Adrasteia with Nemesis, the goddess of vengeance. She personifies society's need for the inevitable punishment of crime. The Orphics considered her an avatar of Ananke, while in the tragic play *Rhesus,* once thought to have been written by Euripides, she is portrayed as the daughter of Zeus.

Adrasteia was also known as the defender of the righteous. One version of the story has her nurturing the infant Zeus in secret in the Dictaean cave in Crete to protect him from his father, Cronus. Adrasteia and her sister Ida, the nymphs of Mount Ida, were the daughters of King Melisseus. The sisters fed the infant milk from the goat Amaltheia. As a reward for their service, Zeus placed the pair in the heavens as the constellations Ursa Major and Minor (the two Bears), along with the goat Amaltheia as Capra.

According to Pausanias, on the mainland of Greece, a spring called Adrasteia was located at the Temple of Nemean Zeus. Her connection with Zeus survives to the modern era in that *Adrastea* is the name of the second by distance, and smallest, of the four inner moons of Jupiter (Zeus).

## AGATHOS DAIMON

Agathos Daimon was a spirit who protected the family and ensured good luck, health, and correct choices in the course of everyday affairs; his name literally means "The Benevolent Spirit."

He was prominent in Greek folk religion and was particularly active in protecting vineyards and crops; it was customary to pour out a few drops of unmixed wine to honor him in every formal banquet. He was the companion of Tyche Agathe (Good Fortune) and was portrayed as a serpent (as spirits often were) or as a young man bearing a bowl in one hand and a serpent wrapped around a poppy or an ear of grain in the other.

## APHRODITE

In Greek mythology, Aphrodite is the goddess of love, beauty, and sexual rapture. According to Hesiod, she was born when Cronus castrated Uranus. When Cronus threw his father's severed genitals into the ocean, the waters began to foam about them. From the sea foam (*aphros*) arose Aphrodite ("She who has arisen from the Sea Foam"), and the sea carried her to either the island Cyprus or the island Cythera. Aphrodite of Cythera represents divine love rather than physical love and is therefore called Aphrodite Urania (The Celestial Aphrodite); Aphrodite Pandemos was the goddess of physical love (desire). The properties of the goddess confirm her similarity with various Eastern deities, such as the Babylonian Ishtar, the Phoenician Ashtarte, and the Egyptian Hathor.

The goddess's priestesses were not prostitutes, but women who represented her in physical form, and sexual intercourse with them was considered simply another method of worship. Her attributes were the dove, the sparrow, the swan, the pomegranate, and the myrtle. She was also sometimes depicted as a goddess of war, especially in Sparta, due to her extramarital affair with Ares, the god of war. In this context Aphrodite is sometimes known as Areia, and the Spartan cult finds a parallel on the island of Cythera, where Aphrodite Urania is depicted armed.

## APOLLO

Apollo is a complex deity who, like Dionysus, originated outside Greece but whose popularity was such that he became one of the most important Olympian gods in ancient Greek and Roman mythology. Portrayed as a beardless, athletic youth, his name most likely means "The Destroyer" (from the Greek verb *apollymi*, to destroy), but with the spread of his cult in Greece, his nature was transformed from destructive to protective.

Apollo was the god of light and the sun, prophecy, healing, music, poetry, and more. He is the son of Zeus and Leto, and has a twin sister, the virgin huntress Artemis. Like his twin, Apollo is an archer. Unlike his twin, who is a primal Greek deity as verified by the archaeological record, Apollo's name is not found in the Mycenaean Linear B tablet archives,* indicating that his cult most likely was embraced by the Greeks shortly after the collapse of civilization in the late Bronze Age.

---

*Linear B is a syllabic script that was used for writing Mycenaean Greek, the earliest attested form of Greek. The script predates the Greek alphabet by many centuries. The oldest Mycenaean Greek writing dates to about 1450 BCE.

At Delphi, Apollo was venerated as the slayer of Python, the earth-dragon, who presided at this cult center of Gaia the Earth, the dragon's mother. His conquest of Delphi earned Apollo the epithet "Pythian," used in the oracular stanzas in this text. In the same light, Apollo controls the casting of the astragalus oracle bones as the god of prophecy. Medicine and healing are also associated with Apollo, for Apollo was

*Statue of the god Apollo*

originally a god who could bring ill-health and deadly plagues, and so could also confer good health. Paean was originally the first physician of the gods; he is an old god whose name is found in the Mycenaean Linear B tablets. Over time, however, "Paean" became an epithet of Apollo, and hymns sung to Apollo were called paeans. As director of the Muses' choir, Apollo also functioned as the patron god of music and poetry.

In Hellenistic times he was more closely identified with Helios, Titan god of the sun, (as his sister Artemis was similarly equated with Selene, Titan goddess of the moon) and drove the fiery chariot of the sun across the sky every passing day. In this respect, Apollo is also called Phoebus, the Radiant One.

## ARES

Ares, the Greek god of war, was tall and handsome but vain, petty, and cruel. Eris (Strife) was his constant companion, and he was also attended by his sons Deimos (Terror) and Phobos (Fear). He is one of the twelve Olympian gods. Zeus is his father and Hera is his mother.

When Ares heard the clash of arms, he rushed onto the battlefield, not caring who won or lost as long as blood was spilt. A sadistic pack followed at his heels: Pain, Panic, Famine, and Oblivion. He was mainly worshipped, and possibly originated, in Thrace, a region peopled by fierce tribes.

Ares embodied the havoc of war and was thus a dangerous force, destructive and unrelenting in battle. In the *Iliad,* his father Zeus tells him: "Of all the gods who dwell on Mount Olympus, you are the most hateful to me, for you enjoy nothing but strife, destruction, and battles." The Greeks questioned his value as a war god because during the Trojan War, Ares was on the losing side, while Athena, the more refined goddess of war, sided with the triumphant Greeks.

Ares' primary role in Greek mythology consisted in his connection to others (mainly his lovers and children). He was well known, for example, as the lover of Aphrodite and father of the many children he had with her.

For all the negative sentiment surrounding this god, however, he was honored throughout Greece. In addition to Thrace, he had major temples in Athens, Sparta, and Olympia. A spring was consecrated to him near Thebes, beneath the temple of Apollo. Moreover, he is an old god, and his name appears in the Bronze Age Linear B tablets both as his own and his epithet Enyalios. Ares' patron animal is the dog, and his bird, the vulture.

## ARTEMIS

Artemis was the twin sister of Apollo and one of the twelve Olympian gods. The daughter of Leto and Zeus, Artemis was the goddess of the wilderness, the hunt and wild animals, and fertility. She is referred to by Homer as Artemis of the Wildland, Mistress of Animals. She is an old god whose name is found in the Bronze Age Mycenaean Linear B tablets. A virgin goddess, she was sometimes identified with Selene (goddess of the moon) and Hecate (goddess of witchcraft). She was the protector of young women, childbirth, and virginity, and was able to both cause and relieve disease in women. Her main vocation was to roam mountains, forests, and uncultivated land hunting for hinds and stags, filtering out the weaker animals and protecting their bloodlines. She was armed with a bow and arrows that were made for her by the smith-god Hephaestus. Thus she was often depicted as a huntress.

One of her main sanctuaries, dedicated to the worship of the bear, was located in Bravrona near Athens. The deer and the cypress were also sacred to her.

## ATHENA

Athena (or Athene, the Roman Minerva) was the virgin goddess of wisdom, war, the arts, industry, justice, and virtue. She was the favorite child of Zeus, having sprung fully grown from her father's head. Her mother was Metis, goddess of wisdom and Zeus's first wife. In fear that

Metis would bear a child mightier than himself, as a prophecy had fore-told, Zeus swallowed his wife whole. In his belly, she began to make a robe and armor for her daughter. The hammering of the helmet caused fierce headaches and he cried out in agony. One of the other gods cleaved Zeus's head with a double-headed Minoan ax. Athena came out fully grown, armed and ready for battle.

One of the epithets of Athena was Pallas. Many interpretations for this have been presented. One story tells us of Pallas and Athena as young girls, and how Athena mistakenly killed her with her javelin and then assumed her name. Another tells us that the goddess slew a giant named Pallas and took his skin to drape over her shield, making her defenses impenetrable (the "aegis"). Finally, Plato makes a connection with the verb *pallein,* "to shake," a reference to the goddess shaking her spear; students of the internal Eastern martial arts will recognize the reference to what the Chinese call *fajin.*\*

Athena Brighteyes is an old goddess, clearly referenced in the Mycenaean Linear B tablets as "The Lady Athena." She represents alkē (αλκή), the ability to fight not only with bravery but with spiritual power as well. In Homer's *Iliad* she repeatedly defeats Ares in hand-to-hand combat. In fact, Zeus, disgusted by Ares' actions, emphatically states to his wife Hera: "Set Athena on him, for she punishes him more often than anyone else does." When, in their final altercation, Athena directly confronts Ares on the battlefield of Troy, she proceeds to mock him:

> "Idiot! You still don't comprehend that I am beyond your power, for you dare to face me!" So saying she struck him on the neck and paralyzed his limbs; and Ares falling took up seven acres of land, and his hair filled with dust, and his armor clattered on the earth.

---

\*Fajin is a term used in the Chinese martial arts, particularly Xingyiquan, T'ai chi ch'uan (Taijiquan), Baguazhang, and Bak Mei. It means to issue or discharge power explosively without pronounced physical movement.

*The Combat of Mars and Minerva*

The artist Joseph-Benoît Suvée (1743–1807) painted a beautiful depiction of this contest in 1771 with *The Combat of Mars and Minerva*. In this canvas, as in the verses of the *Iliad,* Aphrodite is shown trying to drag her lover Ares away from the wrath of Athena Promachos ("She who fights in front lines"); Aphrodite pays the price by subsequently being struck unconscious, but wins the admiration and commendation of Athena in the process.

In his dialogue *Cratylus,* Plato provides a unique outlook on the etymology of the goddess's name, placing words in the mouth of Socrates:

For most [modern interpreters] in their explanations of the poet [Homer], assert that he meant by Athene "mind" (*nous*) and "intelligence" (*dianoia*), and the maker of names appears to have had a singular notion about her; and indeed calls her by a still higher title, "divine intelligence" (*Theou noesis*), as though he would say: This is she who has the mind of God (*Theonoa*).

PLATO, CRATYLUS, 407B,

TRANSLATED BY BENJAMIN JOWETT

Thus, for Plato, her name quite simply means "The Mind of God," a play on words that fits well with the myth of her springing from the head of Zeus fully grown and armored.*

## CRONUS

Cronus, Time, the youngest of the twelve Titans, was the son of Uranus and Gaia. He married his sister Rhea, and their children were Demeter, Hestia, Hera, Hades, Poseidon, and Zeus.

Cronus castrated his father, Uranus, to free his brothers. As a consequence, he and his wife Rhea took the throne. Under their reign, a time of prosperity known as the Golden Age began; people lived without greed, hatred, or violence. But it was fated that Cronus be overthrown by one of his own children. To prevent this from happening, he began to swallow his offspring whole, retaining them inside his belly, where they could do him no harm.

Rhea rebelled, as any mother would, and with the help of the Earth Mother Gaia, she saved her youngest Zeus from this fate. Rhea wrapped a stone in Zeus's swaddling clothes, which Cronus took and immediately swallowed, assuming it was his son. The baby Zeus was then whisked away to Crete, where, in a cave, the goat Amaltheia suckled and raised the infant. When Zeus had grown into a young man, with the help of Gaia, he compelled Cronus to regurgitate the five children he had previously swallowed. Zeus then led the revolt against his father and the dynasty of the Titans, defeating them and banishing them.

---

*For any reader who failed to pick it up, Athena is my favorite god/goddess, representing what is noblest and best in humankind.

## CYBELE

Originally Phrygian, Cybele was the goddess of caverns and the primitive Earth. She ruled over wild beasts and was also goddess of the bees. She was often worshipped on mountaintops. Along with her consort, the vegetation god Attis, Cybele was worshipped in wild, emotional, and often bloody ceremonies.

Because Cybele presided over mountains and fortresses, her crown was in the form of a city wall. The cult of Cybele was directed by eunuch priests, who led the faithful in orgiastic rites accompanied by wild cries and the frenzied music of flutes, drums, and cymbals. Her annual spring festival celebrated the death and resurrection of her beloved Attis.

In Greek mythology her counterpart was the Titaness Rhea, the mother of Zeus. Rhea is often depicted between two lions or on a chariot pulled by lions, and she became known as Rhea Cybele and Magna Mater in Roman times.

## DEMETER

The Greek goddess of the Earth and agriculture (her name literally means "Earth Mother"), she brought forth the fruits of the earth, predominantly the various grains and domestic fruits cultivated by early man. Demeter taught mankind the arts of sowing, plowing, and planting so that they may end their nomadic existence and call one place home. She is also known as Sito, the giver of food (she is referenced as Sito Potnia, the Mistress of Grain, in Mycenaean Greek), and Thesmophoros (*thesmos* means "divine order" or "unwritten law"), steward of agricultural society. In this respect, Demeter was also the creator of organized society and civilization. As a fertility goddess she is often identified with Rhea Cybele and Gaia, Mother Earth.

As both an agricultural goddess and the preserver of divine order, Demeter also presided over the seasons and the cycle of life and death

*The goddess Demeter*

in the natural world. She and her daughter (by Zeus) Persephone were the central figures of the Eleusinian Mysteries, rituals that may be older than the Olympian pantheon.

Persephone (also called Kore, or daughter) was abducted by Hades, King of the Dead, while she played in the fields and was carried off into the underworld. Demeter was beside herself with grief and searched for her far and wide (many of her myths center on this time of sorrow). The seasons paused and nothing would grow on the Earth. Faced with the extinction of all life, Zeus sent his messenger Hermes to the underworld to bring Persephone back. Hades agreed to release her, but on the condition that she had taken nothing from his realm. Persephone, however, had eaten a single pomegranate during her stay. As a condition of eating this fruit, she was bound to Hades for one third of the year, representing the cold winter months. In Greece, it is still a custom during the New Year celebrations to break a pomegranate on the ground, symbolizing the coming release of the Daughter and the end of winter.

## DIONYSUS

Dionysus was the god of wine, agriculture, the fertility of nature, and the patron god of the Greek stage. His worship also epitomizes the dominant features of mystery religions: ecstasy, personal salvation through physical or spiritual intoxication, and initiation into secret rites. It may well be that Dionysus was imported rather late into Greek prehistory from Phrygia or Thrace.

According to one myth, Dionysus was the son of the thunder god Zeus and a mortal woman, Semele. Following her insistence that she be allowed to see Zeus in his true form, Semele was burnt to ashes by his power, with Dionysus still in her womb. Zeus rescued Dionysus, and he underwent a second birth after developing in Zeus's thigh. In another version that formed part of the Orphic religion's mythology, Dionysus, also called Zagreus, was the son of Zeus and Persephone, Queen of the Dead. The Titans lured the infant with toys and then ripped him to shreds, eating everything but his heart, which was saved by Zeus. The Thunderer then remade his son from the heart and implanted him in Semele, who bore the reborn Dionysus-Zagreus. Hence, as in the earlier account, Dionysus is called "twice born."

The bassaris or foxskin was worn by Dionysus in his Thracian mysteries. For this reason, he was sometimes called Bassareus, and his female followers were called Bassarids. Dionysus symbolizes everything chaotic, dangerous and unexpected; he is the protector of those who do not fit in with conventional society.

## EUPHROSYNE OF THE CHARITES

Euphrosyne, whose name means "mirth," was one of the three Graces, or Charites. The Charites were the personification of charm and beauty in nature and in human life. They treasured all things beautiful and bestowed talent upon mortals. Together with the Muses they served as sources of inspiration in the arts. Aglaea ("Splendor") was the youngest, and her elder sisters were Euphrosyne and Thalia ("Good Cheer"). According to Homer, the Charites belonged to the retinue of Aphrodite and her companion Eros. They loved dancing to Apollo's divine music with the Nymphs and the Muses.

According to Greek mythology, the Charites were daughters of Zeus and the Oceanid Eurynome. The Greek poet Pindar states these goddesses were created to fill the world with pleasant moments and good will.

*The three Graces as depicted by Antonio Canova*
*(Photo by Yair Haklai)*

## THE FATES

The Fates are discussed in detail in chapter 1, "How the Ancient Greeks Viewed Fate." The Moirai, or Fates, were the goddesses who controlled the destiny of every person from the time they were born to the time they died. Lachesis, "who assigns lots," decided how much good fortune and time were to be assigned to everyone. Clotho, "the spinner," spun the thread of a person's life. Atropos, "the immoveable one," cut the thread of life when it was time to die.

*The Fates assuming their roles*

## GAIA

Gaia, the Earth or Earth Mother (the primal Greek syllables for "Earth" are *ge, ga, de,* and *da*), was the primordial goddess of the Earth. Gaia was born of Chaos, the great void of emptiness that existed before the creation of the universe. By parthenogenesis, she gave birth to Pontus (the Sea) and to Uranus (the Sky). Gaia took Uranus as her first husband, and their offspring included the Titans, or the "old gods," six sons and six daughters. She also gave birth to the one-eyed Cyclopes, Brontes ("thunderer"), Steropes ("flasher"), and Arges ("brightener"), and to three hundred-handed monsters that became known as the Hecatoncheires.

To protect her children from her husband (he was fearful of their great strength), Gaia hid them. She then asked her youngest son, Cronus, to castrate Uranus, thus severing the union between the Earth and the Sky. To help Cronus achieve his goal, Gaia produced an adamantine sickle as a weapon. Cronus hid nearby until Uranus came to mate with his mother, and as Uranus stood over her, he cut off his father's genitals with the sickle. Blood fell from the severed members to the Earth; from that final union were born the Erinyes (Furies), the Giants, and the Meliae (nymphs).

After the separation of Earth and Sky, Gaia gave birth to other offspring, fathered in turn by the elder Sea God, Pontus.

## HERCULES

Hercules (Herakles) was the most famous Greek hero of ancient times and the most beloved. The son of the Thunderer Zeus and a mortal queen, Alcmene, his name means "the Glory of Hera," Hera being the Queen of the Gods. He was worshipped in many temples all over Greece and Rome, and there are many legends surrounding his exploits.

Extraordinary strength, pronounced physical prowess, and courage were among his prominent attributes. Hercules also used his wits on those occasions when strength would not suffice, such as wrestling the giant Antaeus or tricking Atlas into taking the sky back onto his shoulders. Together with Hermes, he was the protector of gymnastics and wrestling. His iconographic attributes are the lion skin and the club. By conquering dangerous archaic forces, he is said to have made the world safer for mankind and to be its benefactor. Many popular stories were told of his life, the most famous being "The Twelve Labors of Hercules."

## HERMES

Hermes, the herald of the Olympian gods, was the son of Zeus and the nymph Maia, daughter of the Titan Atlas. He was a god of transitions and boundaries; he provided a connection between men and gods as he moved freely between the worlds of the mortal and the Divine—fitting with his role as patron of travelers, shepherds, and merchants. Hermes was also the god of public speaking, literature, athletics, and thievery. He was known for his cunning and shrewdness, outsmarting others both for his own enjoyment and for the sake of humanity. He is also the conductor of souls into the afterlife. Hermes was believed to have invented fire, the lyre (a musical instrument), racing, wrestling, and boxing.

Hermes is an old god and is referenced in the Mycenaean Linear B tablets. He was a very important primal deity worshipped throughout Greece—especially in Arcadia—and possibly throughout the eastern Mediterranean. In classical times Hermes' status was relegated into that of the simple messenger of the gods. His attributes were winged sandals and the *kyrikeion* (caduceus), a symbol of esoteric alchemy embodied by two entwining dragons or snakes that, along with the status of Hermes, degraded into a herald's staff.

In his hymn to Hermes, Homer describes him as

blandly cunning, a robber, a cattle driver, a bringer of dreams, a watcher by night, a thief at the gates, one who was soon to show forth wonderful deeds among the deathless gods.

HYMN 4 TO HERMES,
TRANSLATION BY HUGH G. EVELYN-WHITE

## THE MUSES

The Muses were the Greek goddesses who presided over the arts, especially fine arts, and sciences, including geography and mathematics. They were believed to inspire all artists, especially poets, philosophers, and musicians. Many authors invoked the Muses at the start of their work, calling for help or inspiration. As Homer did in the *Iliad* and the *Odyssey*, poets and musicians invited the Muses to sing through them. They presided over performed metrical speech, *mousikē,* which is where we get the English word *music*. The Muses were the daughters of Zeus and Mnemosyne (Memory). Typically, there is mention of nine muses: Calliope, Clio, Erato, Euterpe, Melpomene, Polyhymnia, Terpsichore, Thalia, and Urania.

*The nine muses and the attributes depicted on a sarcophagus*

## NEMESIS

In Greek mythology, Nemesis was the goddess of divine justice and vengeance. One of the oldest gods, according to Hesiod she was born of Darkness and Night long before Olympian Zeus. She pursues the wicked with the intention of doling out inflexible punishment. The name

*Statue of Nemesis
(Photo by Marshall Astor,
http://creativecommons.org/
licenses/by-sa/2.0)*

*Nemesis* derives from the Greek word νέμειν (némein), meaning "to give what is due"; in this respect, *nemesis* takes on overtones very similar to the Eastern concept of *karma*. Nemesis is portrayed as a remorseless woman with a whip in her left hand, a rope, a sword, or a pair of scales. Nemesis is also called Rhamnusia, from a temple dedicated to her in Rhamnus, a village near Athens. The epithet Adrasteia, "she whom none can escape," properly that of Rhea Cybele, was later applied to her.

## NEREUS

Nereus was the wise "old man of the sea" in Greek myth, the Sea God of the Mediterranean, son of Gaia and Pontus. He was the father of the fifty Nereids, sea-nymphs friendly to man. Nereus was gentle and very wise, and had the power to foretell the future, but would not answer questions unless forced to. To avoid capture, Nereus would change his

*Statue of Nereus, the wise old man of the sea*
*(Photo by Rafael Jiménez from Córdoba, España, http://creativecommons*
*.org/licenses/by-sa/2.0)*

shape and seek to flee. His favorite domain was the Aegean Sea, where many sailors were saved from drowning due to his intervention. Hesiod tells us that he was known for his truthfulness and virtue:

> But the Great Sea was father of truthful Nereus who tells no lies, eldest of his sons. They call him the Old Gentleman because he is trustworthy, and gentle, and never forgetful of what is right, but the thoughts of his mind are mild and righteous.

## NIKE

Nike was the Greek personification of victory. Her Roman equivalent was Victoria. She is one of the most commonly portrayed figures on Greek coins, as everyone likes a good victory. She was the daughter of Pallas and Styx and the sister of Kratos (Strength), Bia (Violence), and

Zelos (Zeal). Nike was a constant companion of Athena and was represented as a woman with wings, dressed in a billowing robe with a wreath or staff. Nike once stood on the outstretched hand of the statue of Athena located in the Parthenon.

Nike is often depicted in her role as divine charioteer, riding her chariot in battle to reward the victorious with glory and fame. Nike and her siblings were also close companions of the thunder god Zeus, whom they sided with in the Olympian gods' war against the Titans.

## POSEIDON

Poseidon Earthshaker was the god of the sea. A son of Cronus and Rhea, the allocation of supreme authority involved him and his brothers, Zeus and Hades, after they had defeated their father, Cronus. Poseidon became ruler of the sea, Zeus ruled the sky, and Hades, the

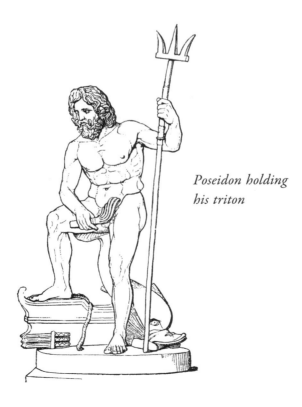

*Poseidon holding his triton*

underworld and the land of the dead. The other attributes of Poseidon involve his role as the god of earthquakes and the god of horses. The symbols associated with him include the dolphin, the horse, and the trident.

Poseidon is an old god; in the Mycenaean Linear B tablets, the name *Poseidon* occurs with greater frequency than does that of Zeus. One of his Bronze Age epithets was Earth-Shaker due to his role in causing earthquakes. He is usually depicted as an older male with curly hair and beard.

# PROMETHEUS

*Titan! to whose immortal eyes*
*The sufferings of mortality,*
*Seen in their sad reality,*
*Were not as things that gods despise;*
*What was thy pity's recompense?*
*A silent suffering, and intense;*
*The rock, the vulture, and the chain,*
*All that the proud can feel of pain.*

"PROMETHEUS" BY LORD BYRON

Prometheus, son of the Titan Iapetus, stole the secret of sacred fire from the gods and gifted it to mankind. In some legends, it was Prometheus himself who fashioned man from clay. His story is tragic. Prometheus would not tell Zeus in prophecy which one of Zeus's sons would eventually overthrow him. In punishment, Zeus chained Prometheus for eternity in the Caucasus Mountains. There, an eagle would eat out his liver, and each day the liver would be regenerated, as the Titan was immortal. The hero Hercules finally pitied the god and killed the bird, thus releasing him.

## THEMIS

Themis was one of the daughters of the Sky, Uranus, and the Earth, Gaia. She was the personification of the divine order of things as sanctioned by universal law. Themis is derived from títhēmi, "to put," and literally means "that which is put in place." Themis represented the place of divine law above human law. She had powers of divination, and it is said that she built the first Oracle at Delphi. Themis is depicted as a stern-looking woman, blindfolded and holding a pair of scales and a cornucopia or sword.

*Blindfolded Themis holding scales in her left hand and a sword in her right*
*(Photo by Alma Pater, www.gnu.org/copyleft/fdl.html)*

## TRITON

Triton was the son of the god of the sea, Poseidon, and goddess of the sea, Amphitrite, and lived with them in a golden palace under the sea. He rode the waves on horses and carried a conch shell, upon which he blew either violently or gently to stir up or calm the waves. He could blow it so loudly that it could scare away the giants, who thought it was the roar of a wild beast. Triton is represented as having the upper body of a man and the tail of a fish—the original merman.

According to the story of the Argonauts, Triton's home was on the coast of Libya. The story goes that when the *Argo* was driven ashore in the Gulf of Sirte in Libya the crew carried the vessel for twelve days to reach Lake Tritonis, a mythical body of water in the Sahara; according to the historian Herodotus, the lake contained two islands. Triton welcomed the Argonauts with the gifts of earth and water and guided them through the lake's marshy outlet back to the Mediterranean.*

Triton's daughter Pallas was killed by his foster daughter Athena during a fight between the two goddesses, after which Athena assumed her name in tribute.

## TYCHE

Tyche was originally the goddess of fortune and chance, and evolved into the goddess of prosperity. Many Greek cities choose her as their protector. She is regarded as a daughter of Zeus according to Pindar and as a daughter of Oceanus and Tethys according to Hesiod. Tyche

---

*What was once thought to be pure epic fantasy took on a different light with the discovery of "The Cave of Swimmers," a cavern with ancient rock art in the mountainous Gilf Kebir plateau of the Libyan Sahara. The cave and rock art were discovered in October 1933 by the Hungarian explorer László Almásy and contains Neolithic pictographs (rock painting images) of people swimming. They are estimated to have been created ten thousand years ago.

is often associated with Nemesis and with Agathos Daimon (The Benevolent Spirit). She was portrayed with a cornucopia, a rudder of destiny, and a wheel of fortune.

*Relief depicting three versions of the goddess Tyche*

## ZEPHYRUS

Zephyrus was the Greek god of the west wind, the gentlest of the winds. He was believed to live in a cave in Thrace. He is the brother of Boreas (the North Wind), Eurus (the East Wind), and Notus (the

*Statue of Zephyrus.*
*(Photo by Yair Haklai, http://creativecommons.org/licenses/by-sa/3.0.)*

South Wind); together they make up the Anemoi, the gods of the winds. He was also both the brother and lover of Iris, the goddess of the rainbow, and Chloris, the goddess of flowers. Zephyrus represents the fructifying breeze and is the messenger of spring.

## ZEUS, GOD OF THUNDER

Zeus, the youngest son of the Titans Cronus and Rhea, was the supreme ruler of the pantheon of gods who resided on Mount Olympus. As the supreme celestial deity, Zeus oversaw the conduct of civilized life, but he was originally worshipped as a god of the weather by the early Greek tribes. His main attribute was the thunderbolt, and he commanded thunder, lightning, and rain. His name is composite, expressed as both Zeus (the "Joiner") and Dias (the "Divider"), Dias-Zeus. Zeus's other attributes were the scepter, the eagle, and the aegis, which was the skin of Amaltheia, the goat who suckled him as an infant.

Cronus and Rhea had several children—Hestia, Demeter, Hera, Hades, and Poseidon—but Cronus swallowed them all as soon as they were born, because of a prophecy from Gaia (Earth) and Uranus (Sky) that he was destined to be overcome by his own son in turn as he had overthrown his own father.

Rhea sought Gaia's counsel to devise a plan to save Zeus from the fate of his siblings. Cronus deserved retribution for his acts against Uranus and his own children. They devised a plan to hand Cronus a rock wrapped in swaddling clothes instead of the baby. When Rhea gave birth to Zeus in Crete, Cronus promptly and unknowingly swallowed the false baby. When Zeus was grown, he forced Cronus to expel first the stone and then his siblings. Together, Zeus and his brothers and sisters overthrew Cronus and the other Titans. Zeus took Hera as his queen and ruled in Heaven.

During the time of Great Kings, Zeus was the protector of the monarch and his family. But when the age of kings evolved into democracy, he became the chief arbitrator and peacemaker of both gods and men. Zeus was commonly known as Kosmetas ("who brings order"), Soter ("savior"), Polios ("guardian of the city"), and Eleutherios ("guarantor of political freedoms"). In this text, moreover, you will find his name used with other epithets, describing his many functions in Greek religion.

## ZEUS AMMON

Ammon was the Greek name of an Egyptian oracular god whose main sanctuary was at Siwa oasis deep in the Libyan Desert. Originally, this was the site where Libyan tribes worshipped a god who had taken the

*Statue of Zeus Ammon;*
*note the curled horns on the back of his head.*

shape of a ram. He may have been related to Baal Hammon, a god venerated by the Semitic peoples (i.e., the Phoenicians and Carthaginians).
This cult was taken over by Egyptian priests, who identified the god
with their supreme deity Amun. The first Greeks to visit the shrine
called the god Zeus Ammon. His cult readily spread to the Greek world
and was especially propagated by the poet Pindar (522–445 BCE),
one of the first Greeks to erect a statue to the god. But Zeus Ammon
became most famous because Alexander the Great claimed to be his son
and often wore crowns sporting the horns of Ammon.

# THE MIND SHAPES ALL

## Consorting with the Past, Present, and Future

At the risk of becoming tiring, I will ask again: why did people believe in, and continue to believe in, divination and cleromancy? Is it simply fear for the morrow, as stated earlier? Is it the mind playing tricks on us, a fraud and a charade? If so, why is it that, for many of us, cleromancy oracles (for example, the Chinese I Ching) seem to answer our questions with surprising accuracy, often replying as if they had full awareness of our circumstances, repeatedly advising us with absolute, statistically provoking success?

I have a possible explanation for this dilemma.

In Crete, on the peninsula of Akrotiri near Hania, there are two Orthodox monasteries situated closely to each other. There is Moni Katholikou, an older, deserted one close to the seashore, built in the sixth century CE and abandoned centuries later due to pirate raids. Moni Gouvernetou is the newer one higher up on the hillside, built in the twelfth century by monks of the earlier monastery who wanted a more defendable location.

Three hundred yards down a steep path from Moni Gouvernetou is a large cave inside of which is built a small church. The true depth of the cave is unknown, because most of it has yet to be charted in our generation. One striking thing about it is the large stalactite in its entrance chamber, which has the unmistakable shape of a bear. Perhaps even more interesting is that archaeological excavations have shown that the cave has a religious history. Neolithic man worshipped the Earth Bear and the Mother Goddess there. In Minoan Crete around the seventeenth century BCE, the cave became a temple to Diktynna, a virgin Cretan goddess whose totem was the bear. She was followed by her classical Greek counterpart Artemis, another virgin deity to whom the bear was sacred, and who in Roman times became Diana. When the Greeks eventually converted to Christianity (between the fourth and sixth centuries CE), the cave became a temple to the Virgin Mary of the Bears (Panagia Arkoudiotissa), and a baptismal font was built onto the stalactite, fed by the steady drip of a small spring. Hence the goddess worshipped in the cave changed her name, but not her essence, throughout the millennia, something that I personally believe holds true for many aspects of Greek culture.

In the courtyard of Moni Gouvernetou, over the entrance to a small chapel, there is a startling inscription that is more reminiscent of Zen Buddhism than Greek Orthodoxy: "Mind is That which Shapes All and

*The inscription from Moni Gouvernetou*

the Reason for All Being." The inscription can be seen in the image on page 44. This quote is suggestive of the philosophy of Anaxagoras, and, once again, proof of the great extent of ancient thought that filtered into Orthodoxy, despite the best efforts of church authorities to the contrary. It is most likely that this same axiom, in this most sanctified of places, was passed by word of mouth, from shaman to shaman, from shaman to priest, and hence from priest to priest, from Paleolithic times until today! It is on Mind, then, that I would like to concentrate my efforts.

The *collective unconscious* is a term introduced by the psychiatrist Carl Jung to represent a form of the unconscious mind common to humanity as a whole, and originating in the innate anatomy of the brain. The structure of our space-time continuum has been characterized with great success by modern physics and can be broadly depicted in summary as shown in the diagram below. What if our own consciousness followed this same structure, as Jung himself imagined? Would it be possible, then, for consciousness to be depicted with the same symbolism?

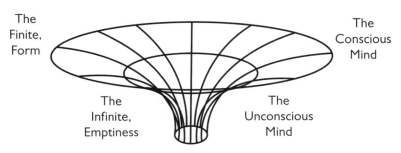

*Structure of our space-time continuum.*

The philosopher Plato himself once wrote, in his *Philebus* (16c): "The finite and infinite are inherent in man." Perhaps this great sage was aware of something that we are missing today. The structure inherent in the space-time continuum, which is based on modern astrophysics, could explain much of the so-called paranormal and psychic phenomena recorded in the literature. A part of our Mind, our unconscious self, extends into the autonomic nervous system of our bodies, and from there—as I believe—into our very cells. If one accepts the concept of a collective unconscious as proposed by Jung, then this mass unconscious must exist somewhere beyond space and time, like a black hole orbiting a star. Essentially, one part of our Mind is interconnected in the area of the Infinite, and we are all like the fingers of one hand, united at the palm—we would like to think that we are individual entities, but in essence one part of ourselves comprises a whole.

Calming our thoughts, fixing our breath in the center of our bellies, concentrating on the query that is foremost in our mind, we dive deep into the waters of the unconscious Mind with every toss of the astragali. We converse with Clotho and shyly touch the feet of Lachesis, attempting to convince them to intercede on our behalf, before their little sister, Atropos, the Inflexible One, makes our state of affairs permanent in space and time. In the realm of our unconscious Mind, as in the black hole of modern astrophysics, space and time are compacted and nonlinear. The past (Lachesis) consorts with the present (Clotho), and both run into the future together (Atropos). Diving into Mind, then, tossing the astragali, we reach the borders of Ananke herself (Necessity, Karma), the Mother of all three Fates, and touch upon the primordial reasons for unfolding events.

It is there, at that instant of tossing the bones, symbols of the impermanence of our lives, that we hear the voice of Lightbearer Apollo, guiding us with such choices as must be made.

# PART II

# Interpreting the Oracle
## Guidance, Inspiration, and Insight

Οἵδε χρησμοὶ Ἀπόλλωνος Πυθίου ἐνὶ πέντε
    ἀστραγάλοις,
τοῦ χρή αἰεί φωνῆς ἐπακοῦσαι.

The prophecies of Pythian Apollo,
whose voice you are obliged to obey,
are found in the toss of the five astragali.

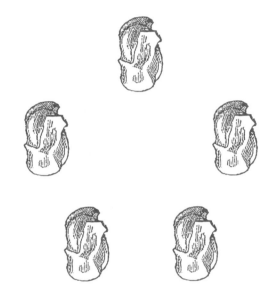

**ΛΛΛΛΛ** (bones) — **11111** (coins)

Total Value: 5

Διὸς Ὀλυμπίου

Olympian Zeus

# OLYMPIAN ZEUS

*Πάντες ὁμοῦ χεῖοι, Φοίβου φωνῆς ἐπάκουσον.*
*Ζεὺς σωτὴρ ἀγαθὴν βουλὴν σαῖσι φρεσὶ*
    *δώσει,*
*δώσει δ' εὐφροσύνην καὶ δώσει πάνθ' ὅσ' ἂν*
    *εὔχῃ·*
*ἀλλ' Ἀφροδείτην εἰλάσκου καὶ Μαιάδος υἱόν.*

All throws are ones, hear the voice of the Shining
    One.
Zeus Savior will inspire you;
He will give you happiness and all that you wish for.
But sing the praises of Aphrodite and Hermes, son
    of Maia.

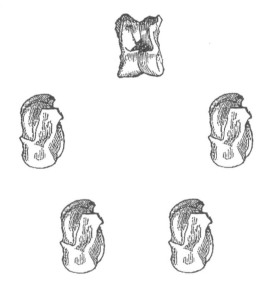

**ΛΛΛΛΓ** (bones) — **11113** (coins)

Total Value: 7

*Ἀθηνᾶς Ἀρείας*

Athena Who Judges

# ATHENA WHO JUDGES

*Τέσσαρες εἰ μοῦνοι καὶ εἷς τρεῖος, τάδε
    φράζει·
ἔχθραν καὶ κακότητα φυγών ἤξεις ποτ' ἐς
    ἆθλα·
ἤξεις καὶ σώσει σὲ θεὰ γλαυκῶπις Ἀθήνη,
βουλὴ δ' ἔσται σοὶ καταθύμιος, ἣν ἐπιβάλλῃ.*

Four ones and a three command the following:
By avoiding Enmity and Hatred, you will attain your
    reward.
Reaching this journey's end, you will be saved by
    Athena Brighteyes.
Her judgment, which she imposes, will be for you
    welcome.

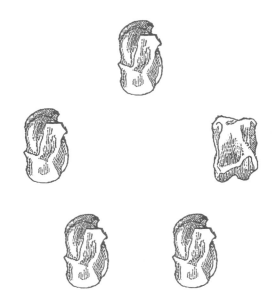

**ΛΛΛΛᐃ** (bones) — **11114** (coins)

Total Value: 8

*Μοιρῶν*

The Fates

# THE FATES

Τέσσαρα δ᾽ εἷς πείπτων καὶ μοῦνοι τέσσαρες
    ἑξῆς,
πρᾶξιν μὴ πράξῃς, ἢν πράσσεις, οὐ γὰρ
    ἄμεινον·
ἀμφὶ δὲ κάμνοντος χαλεπὸν καὶ ἀμήχανον
    ἔσται·
δεῖ δὲ ἀπόδημον ἱκέσθαι νῦν, χρόνῳ οὐ κακὸν
    ἔσται.

A single four falls, and four ones:

Do not act upon that which you now pursue, for it
    will not be good;

He who tries will find the task both difficult and
    impossible.

For now, you must travel abroad; the future,
    however, hides no evil.

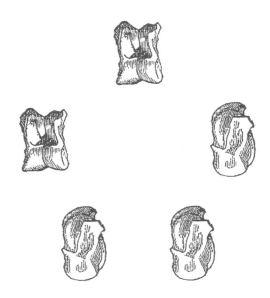

**ΓΓΛΛΛ** (bones) — **33111** (coins)

Total Value: 9

Ἀετοῦ Διὸς

The Eagle of Zeus

# THE EAGLE OF ZEUS

*Εἰ δὲ κὲ πείπτωσιν δύο τρεῖοι, τρεῖς δ' ἅμα*
  *μοῦνοι,*
*ἀετὸς ὑψιπέτης ἐπὶ δεξιὰ χειρὸς ὁδείτη·*
*δώσει μαντείαν ἀγαθήν· σὺν Ζηνὶ μεγίστῳ*
*τεύξῃ ἐφ ἣν ὁρμᾷς πρᾶξιν· μηθὲν δὲ φοβηθῇς.*

Two threes fall, and three ones:
The high-flying Eagle will guide you to the right
  hand.
Your fortune will be positive; with great Zeus's aid,
You will succeed in what you strive for with passion.
  Fear nothing.

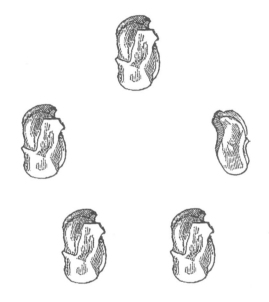

**ΓΔΔΔΔ** (bones) — **61111** (coins)

Total Value: 10

Δαίμονος Μεγίστου

The Great Spirit

# THE GREAT SPIRIT

*Εἷς ὢν ἐξείτης καὶ μοῦνοι τέσσαρες ὄντες·*
*δαίμονι ἥντιν' ἔχεις εὐχὴν ἀποδόντι σοὶ ἔσται*
*βέλτειον, εἰ μέλλεις πράσσειν κατὰ νοῦν ἃ*
*    μεριμνᾷς.*
*Δημήτηρ γὰρ σοὶ καὶ Ζεῦς σωτῆρες ἔσονται.*

One six and four ones come to you:
The god who has blessed you will grant you the best
    of outcomes
if you act upon that which you have in your mind.
Demeter and Zeus will be your saviors.

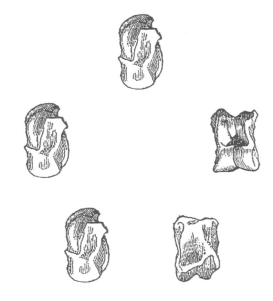

**ΑΑΑΔΓ** (bones) — **11143** (coins)

Total Value: 10

Τύχης Εὐδαίμονος

Tyche, Opportune Chance

# TYCHE, OPPORTUNE CHANCE

*Εἰ δὲ κὲ τρεῖς μοῦνοι, εἶς τέσσαρα, τρία ὁ*
*    πέμπτος,*
*τὴν πρᾶξιν σὺ γὲ μὴ πράξῃς, ἣν νῦν ἐπιβάλλῃ·*
*νῦν τ᾽ ἐν νούσῳ ἐόντα θεοὶ κατέχουσι*
*    σεαυτὸν·*
*τὸν τὲ πόνον λύσουσίν σοι καὶ οὐθὲν κακὸν*
*    ἔσται.*

If there are three ones, one four, the fifth a three:
Do not proceed with that which is imposed on you.
Now, though you are in sadness, the gods will guide
    you;
They will deliver you from suffering, and there will
    be no evil.

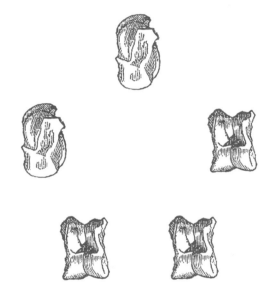

**ΓΓΓΔΔ** (bones) — **33311** (coins)

Total Value: 11

Νείκης

Nike, Goddess of Victory

# NIKE, GODDESS OF VICTORY

*Εἰ δὲ κὲ τρεῖς τρία πείπτωσιν, χεῖοι δὲ δύ᾽*
   *ἄλλοι,*
*πράγματα λήψῃς δ᾽ ἃ θέλεις, ἅπαντά σοί*
   *ἐστι·*
*ἐὰν τειμιτὸν σὲ τὸ θεῖον, πάντων τὲ*
   *κρατήσεις·*
*βουλὴ δ᾽ ἔσται σοὶ καταθύμιος, ἢν ἐπιβάλλῃ.*

If three threes fall, and the remaining two are ones:
You will accomplish what you desire, all is yours.
If you honor the gods, you will triumph.
The judgment they impose will be welcome to you.

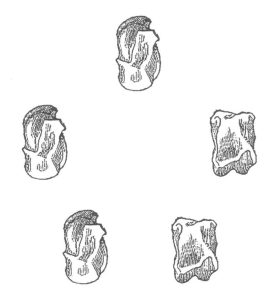

**Λ Λ Λ Δ Δ** (bones) — **11144** (coins)

Total Value: 11

Ἀρτέμιδος Βραυρωνίας

Artemis of Bravrona

# ARTEMIS OF BRAVRONA

*Χείους τρεῖς ὁράας καὶ τέσσαρα λοιπὸν*
*ἐπόντα·*
*εἰς ἄνεμον σπείρειν, εἰς πέτραν σπέρματα*
*βάλλειν,*
*χειμερίοις αὔραις πεφύλαξο σὺ πόντον*
*ἐπιπλεῖν·*
*ἥσυχα βουλεύου καὶ ἐναντίος ἵστασο τούτων.*

You see three ones, the rest are fours:

Do not sow into the wind, nor plant seeds in hard
stone.

Do not sail on deep oceans during the storms of
winter.

Contemplate quietly, and remain unaffected by all
this.

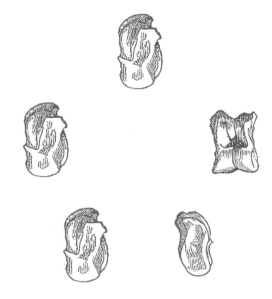

**ΛΛΛΓⵎ** (bones) — **11136** (coins)

Total Value: 12

*Διονύσου Βασσαρέως*

Dionysus Bassareus

# DIONYSUS BASSAREUS

*Εἷς μόνος ἐξείτης, εἷς τρεῖος, καὶ μοῦνοι τρεῖς*
*   ὄντες·*
*οἰνάνθην μὴ σπεῦδε τρυγᾶν μηδ' αἰρινὰ*
*   σοῖκα,*
*μηδ' ἀκονᾶν μόλυβον βούλου, μὴ κῦμα*
*   βαρύνειν·*
*ἄλλο τί μαστεύειν σὲ χρεών, τούτου δὲ*
*   λαθέσθαι.*

One lone six, one three, and three ones fall:
Be in no hurry to harvest the buds of the vine, nor
   the summer figs,
nor should you prepare your weights for the line,*
   for you will lie heavy in the waves.
Your obligation lies elsewhere, and it eludes you.

---

*The verse refers to lead weights used for fishing.

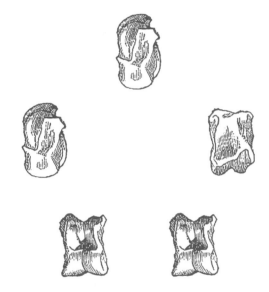

**ΑΑΓΓΔ** (bones) — **11334** (coins)

Total Value: 12

Ζηνὸς Βασιλῆος

Zeus the King

# ZEUS THE KING

*Χεῖοι δύο μὲν εἰσί, τρεῖοι δύο, εἷς τέσσαρα·*
*ἐνχείρει, πράξεις γὰρ ἀνελπίστως ἃ προαιρῇ·*
*καὶ τὰ φόβον γὰρ ἔχοντα χαρὰν κέρδος τὲ*
*προδηλοῖ.*
*Ζῆνα μέγαν βασιλῆα σέβου καὶ Φοῖβον*
*ἄνακτα.*

Two ones fall, two threes, and a four:
Proceed. You will achieve your goals beyond your
    wildest dreams.
And those things that seem fearful, the god decrees
    will bring you joy.
Honor the great king, Zeus, and Lord Apollo
    Lightbearer.

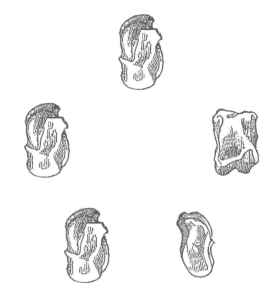

**ΛΛΛ⸤Δ** (bones) — **11164** (coins)

Total Value: 13

Ἑρμοῦ Παιγνίου

Hermes of the Games

# HERMES OF THE GAMES

*Εἷς ὢν ἐξείτης, τρεῖς χεῖοι, τέσσερα ὁ*
  *πέμπτος·*
*ὦ ξέν, ἐπ' ἐμπορίαν ἀγαθῶς ἴξῃ ἀπόδημος·*
*καιρὸν μὴ ζήτει· τεύξει θεὸς ὥστε χαρῆναι,*
*οὐ γὰρ δύσκολόν ἐστι φέρει καρποὺς τὲ τὸ*
  *πρᾶγμα.*

One six, three ones, the fifth is a four:
Stranger, your business in foreign lands will go well.
Do not seek for opportunity; the god will arrange
    for your happiness.
For it is not difficult for this situation to bring you
    gains.

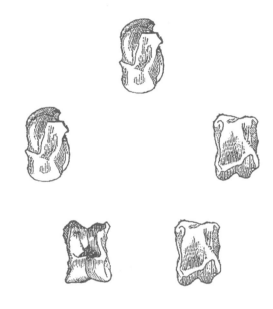

ΛΛΓΔΔ (bones) — 11344 (coins)

Total Value: 13

Μουσῶν Ἡδυεπειῶν

The Melodious Muse

# THE MELODIOUS MUSE

*Εἰ δὲ κὲ εἷς μέν τρεῖος, δύο μοῦνοι καὶ δύο*
   *τέσσαρα,*
*εὖ πράξεις· ἔσται καὶ εὔοδα καὶ πολυκερδῆ·*
*κοινωνεῖν δὴ ἄμεινον ἀπεργασίας ἐπιχιρῖν·*
*κρυπτομένων δ᾽ ἀνύειν ἔχε Μουσῶν*
   *ἡδυεπειῶν.*

If one three falls, two ones, and two fours:
You would do well to act. Good prospects, profits
   easily gained.
It is better now to participate, rather than to try to
   create.
Keep private, in order to succeed, the sweet verse of
   the Muse.

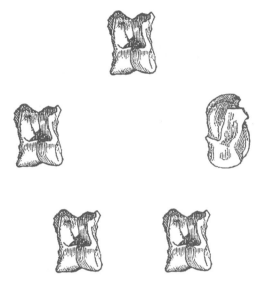

**ΓΓΓΓΛ** (bones) — **33331** (coins)

Total Value: 13

Θέμιδος

Themis

# THEMIS

*Μοῦνος δ᾽ εἷς πείπτων καὶ τρεῖοι τέσσαρες*
*ἐξῆς·*
*ὁδὸς ἄκαρπος καὶ ἀμήχανος, μὴ σπεύδεις νῦν*
*δέ·*
*βουλὴν ἣν πράσσεις θεὸς οὐκ ἐᾷ· ἀλλ᾽*
*ἀνάμεινον·*
*δεινὸν δὲ εἰς ἔριν ἔρχεσθαι καὶ ἀγῶνα δίκην*
*δέ.*

A single one falls, and four threes:
This road has no gains for you and is impassable. Be
   in no hurry at present.
The god will not allow that which you pursue; you
   must wait.
It is distressing to enter into conflict and legal trials.

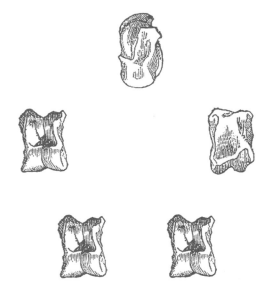

**ΛΓΓΓΔ** (bones) — **13334** (coins)

Total Value: 14

Τρίτωνος

Triton

# TRITON

*Εἶς χεῖος καὶ τρεῖς τρεῖοι καὶ τέσσαρ' ὁ*
  *πέμπτος·*
*λακτίζεις πρὸς κέντρα, πρὸς ἀντία κύματα*
  *μοχθεῖς·*
*ἰχθὺν ἐν πελάγει ζητεῖς· μὴ σπεῦδ' ἐπὶ*
  *πρᾶξιν·*
*οὔ σοι χρήσιμόν ἐστι θεοὺς βιάσασθαι*
  *ἀκαίρως.*

A single one and three threes, the fifth a four:

Your attempts are in vain; you struggle against the
  waves.

You seek a fish in the ocean; be in no hurry to act.

Nor is it useful for you to make demands of the gods
  at the wrong time.

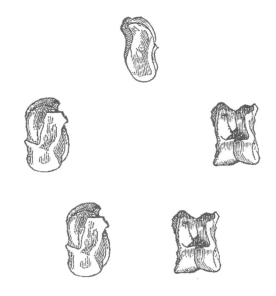

# ΓΑΛΓΓ (bones) — 61133 (coins)

## Total Value: 14

Ἑρμοῦ Διάκτορος

Hermes the Guide

# HERMES THE GUIDE

Εἶς ὢν ἐξείτης, δύο μοῦνοι καὶ δύο τρεῖοι,
μήτε σὺ φρικτὰ νόει μήτ᾽ ἀντία δαίμονος
   ἔρχου
δεινὰ φρονῶν· οὐθὲν γὰρ ὀνήσιμον ἔστιν ἀπ᾽
   αὐτοῦ·
οὐδ ὁδὸν ἣν στείχεις, κέρδος τί σοὶ ἐστιν ἀπ᾽
   αὐτῆς.

One six, two ones, and two threes:
Do not reflect upon evil, nor go against the god,
planning calamities, for there is nothing useful in
   this.
Neither on the path you are taking, will you uncover
   gain in the end.

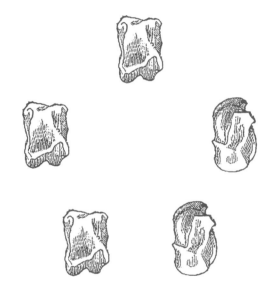

**△ △ △ △ △** (bones) — **44411** (coins)

Total Value: 14

*Ἀγαθοῦ Δαίμονος*

The Benevolent Spirit*

---

*Agathos Daimon, the Benevolent Spirit, is often associated with Tyche, or Fortune.

# THE BENEVOLENT SPIRIT

*Εἰ δὲ κὲ πείπτωσιν τρία τέσσαρα καὶ δύο*
  *μοῦνοι,*
*ἡγεμονεύσει σοὶ δαίμων ὁδόν, ἢν ἐπιβάλλῃ,*
*πένψει δ' εἰς ἀγαθὸν σὲ φιλομμειδὴς*
  *Ἀφροδείτη,*
*πολλοῖς σὺν καρποῖς στείξεις καὶ ἀπήμονι*
  *μοίρῃ.*

Should three fours fall and two ones:
The god will lead you down the path he imposes.
Smiling Aphrodite will guide you with benevolence;
Your path will be productive, and no clouds hang
    over your fate.

**Α Γ Γ Δ Δ** (bones) — **13344** (coins)

Total Value: 15

Διὸς Σωτῆρος

Zeus the Savior

# ZEUS THE SAVIOR

*Εἷς χεῖος, τρεία πείπτοντες δύο, τέσσαρα*
    *δοιά·*
*ἢν ἐπιβάλλῃ νῦν πρᾶξιν, θαρρῶν ἴθι, πρᾶσσε·*
*ἐνχείρει, καλὰ γὰρ μαντεῖα θεοὶ τάδ' ἔφηναν·*
*μηδὲ πονεῖν ἀλέου· οὐθὲν γὰρ σοὶ κακὸν*
    *ἔσται.*

A single one, two threes fall, and two fours:

For such deeds as must transpire, with courage, take
    action.

Proceed, for the gods send good tidings on this
    matter.

Spare no efforts; there is nothing evil ahead for you.

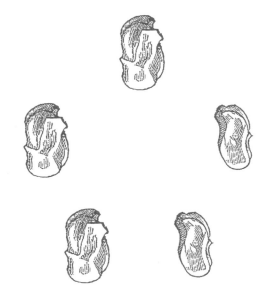

**ΛΛΛΓΓ** (bones) — **11166** (coins)

Total Value: 15

Διὸς Ἄμμωνος

Zeus Ammon

# ZEUS AMMON

*Εἰ δὲ κὲ πείπτωσιν μοῦνοι τρεῖς καὶ δύο*
  *ξεῖται,*
*ἣν φρεσὶν ὁρμαίνεις ὁδόν, εἰς ταύτην ἴθι*
  *θαρρῶν,*
*πᾶν δὲ θεὸς δώσει· πράξεις δ' ὅσα θυμὸς*
  *ἀνώγει*
*πάντα, Ζεὺς δ' ὑψιβρεμέτης σωτὴρ σοὶ*
  *ἐπέσαι.*

If three ones fall and two sixes:
On that path which inspires you, walk boldly ahead.
The god will grant you everything; proceed as your
  inspiration commands.
Zeus, who thunders in the heights, will be your
  savior.

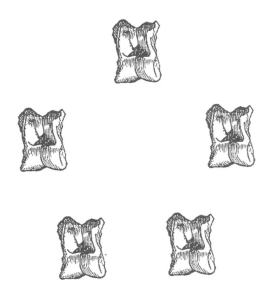

**ΓΓΓΓΓ** (bones) — **33333** (coins)

Total Value: 15

Τύχης Ἀγαθῆς

Benevolent Fortune

# BENEVOLENT FORTUNE

*Εἰ πάντες τρεῖοι, Φοίβου φωνῆς ἐπάκουσον·*
*ἤ τὲ τεκοῦσα βρέφος ξηροὺς μαστοὺς ἔχει*
   *ἄμφω,*
*ἀλλὰ πάλιν βλάστησε καὶ ἄφθονον ἔσχε*
   *γάλακτος·*
*καὶ τότε πάντα καλῶς ἕξεις περὶ ὧν μ᾽*
   *ἐπερωτᾷς.*

Should all throws be threes, then hear the voice of
   the Shining One.
She who has borne a child, found both her breasts dry.
But lo, she has flowered once again and has milk
   aplenty;
And all will be well for you, concerning that which
   you ask of me.

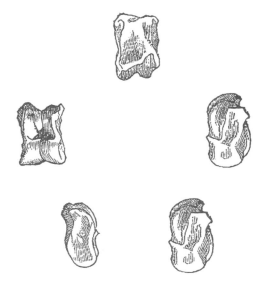

**ΔΓϹΛΛ** (bones) — **43611** (coins)

Total Value: 15

Διὸς Ξενίου

Zeus the Guardian of Travelers

# ZEUS THE GUARDIAN OF TRAVELERS

*Τετρῶος, τὲ καὶ τρεῖος καὶ ξεῖθος καὶ δύο*
  *μοῦνοι·*
*πρᾶξιν ἐφ ἦν μέλλεις, μὴ σπεῦδ', οὔπω γὰρ ὁ*
  *καιρός·*
*καὶ ἐν νούσῳ σὲ γ' ἐόντα θεοὶ σώζουσιν*
  *ἑτοίμως,*
*καὶ τὸν ἐν ἄλλῃ χώρᾳ ὁδοῦ λήξειν θεὸς αὐδᾷ.*

One four, one three, one six, and two ones:
Concerning that which you strive for, be patient,
    it is not yet time.
And should the gods present you with sadness,
    they will redeem you willingly.
He who is in foreign lands will complete his
    journey, says the god.

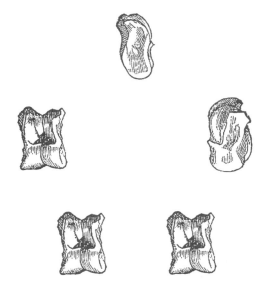

**ⅭⅭⅭⅭⲀ** (bones) — **63331** (coins)

Total Value: 16

Ἡρακλέους

Hercules

# HERCULES

*Εἷς ξεῖτος καὶ τρεῖς τρεῖοι καὶ μοῦνος ὁ*
  *πέμπτος·*
*οὔπω καιρός, ἄγαν σπεύδεις δὲ σύ, μὴ κενὰ*
  *παράξῃς·*
*μηδ' ὥς τίς τε λέων τυφλὴν ἐκύησε λοχείην·*
*ἥσυχα βουλεύου καὶ σοὶ θεὸς ἡγεμονεύσει.*


One six, three threes, the fifth a one:
It is not yet time, be in no hurry; do not act
    foolishly.
Be not like the lioness that bore a den of blind cubs.*
Prepare yourself calmly, and the god will guide you.

---

*This same wording is also found in the verse dedicated to "Benevolent Time"; its duplication is not an error but reflects what was found in the archaeological record as per Heinevetter's thesis. When compiling the final oracular stanzas, we were faced with the difficult choice of retaining or revising it, but chose to retain the verse as found, considering revision of the wording to be hubris.

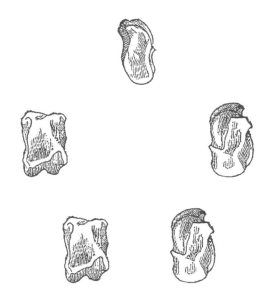

**⊏ΔΔΔ** (bones) — **64411** (coins)

Total Value: 16

Κυβέλης

Cybele

## CYBELE

*Εἷς ξεῖθος καὶ τεσσάρεοι δύο καὶ δύο μοῦνοι·*
*ξηρῶν ἀπὸ κλάδων καρπὸν οὐκ ἔσται λαβεῖν·*
*ὅταν ἀμελήσῃς σεαυτόν, αἰὼν ἀβίωτος·*
*οὐκ ἔστι μὴ σπείραντα θερίσαι κάρπιμα.*

One six, two fours, and two ones:
From dry branches one cannot harvest fruit.
Neglect your own self, and life becomes unlivable.
Neither is it possible to reap bountiful fruit, when
    you have not sown.

**ΛΓΔΔΔ** (bones) — **13444** (coins)

Total Value: 16

Προμηθέως

Prometheus

# PROMETHEUS

*Εἷς μοῦνος, εἷς τρεῖος, καὶ τέσσαρ' οἱ λοιποί·*
*ὑπόσχεσιν τὸ πρᾶγμα γενναίαν ἔχει·*
*χρυσοῦν ποιήσεις χρησμὸν ἐπιτυχών, ξένε·*
*ψῆφον δικαίαν τήνδε παρὰ θεῶν ἔχεις.*

A single one, one three, the rest are fours:
The circumstances promise great reward.
If you act wisely on what the divination tells you,
    stranger, you will succeed;
From the gods, you have just approval for that which
    you seek.

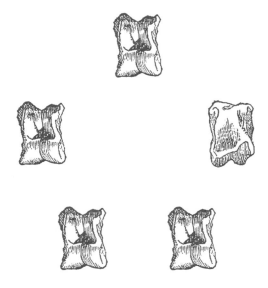

# ΓΓΓΓΔ (bones) — 33334 (coins)

## Total Value: 16

*Γῆς καρποφόρου*

## The Fertile Earth

# THE FERTILE EARTH

*Εἶς τετρῶος καὶ τρεῖοι πάντες ἐφεξῆς,*
*ἄπαντα πράξεις καὶ διοικήσεις καλῶς·*
*βοηθὸν ἕξεις μετὰ τύχης τὸν Πύθιον·*
*γῆ σοὶ τέλειον καρπὸν ἀποδώσει πόνοις.*

Should a single four fall and all the rest threes,
then you will succeed in all things, and command
    capably.
Along with luck, you will have the aid of Apollo.
The Earth will bear you perfect fruit for your labors.

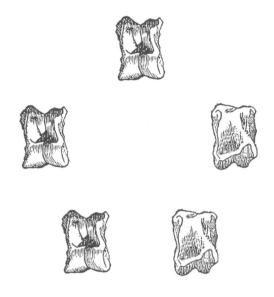

**ΓΓΓΔΔ** (bones) — **33344** (coins)

Total Value: 17

Νηρέως

Nereus

# NEREUS

*Εἰ δὲ κὲ τρεῖς οἱ τρεῖοι καὶ δύο οἱ τεσσάρεοι·*
*κύμασι μάχεσθαι χαλεπόν· ἀνάμεινον, φίλε·*
*μοχθεῖν ἀνάνκη· μεταβολὴ δ' ἔσται καλή·*
*ζάλην μεγίστην φεῦγε, μὴ τι καὶ βλαβῆς.*

The threes are three, the fours are two:
It is difficult to fight against the waves. Stay, friend;
Hard labor is necessary. Changes will be good.
Avoid extreme turmoil, for you may suffer evil.

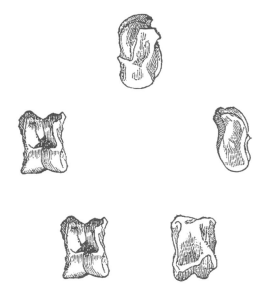

**ΑΓΓΔⵣ** (bones) — **13346** (coins)

Total Value: 17

Ἀρτέμιδος Ἀγρότηρας

Artemis of the Fields

# ARTEMIS OF THE FIELDS

*Ξεῖθος, μοῦνος, εἷς τέσσαρα, τρεῖοι οἱ λοιποὶ.*
*Λαγὼς διελθὼν πάντα σημαίνει καλῶς.*
*Λύπης πέπαυσο· προσδέχου λοιπὸν χαράν.*
*Τειμῶν τὸ θεῖον τὴν συνείδησιν τρέφεις.*

One six, a single one, one four, the rest are threes:
When a rabbit happens by, then all will go well.
Cease your suffering, for happiness awaits you.
By honoring the gods, you will nourish your
   consciousness.

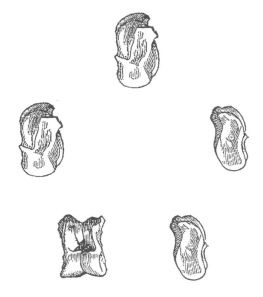

Λ Λ Γ Ϲ Ϲ (bones) — 11366 (coins)

Total Value: 17

Δήμητρος Καρποφόρου

Fruit-bearing Demeter

# FRUIT-BEARING DEMETER

*Δύο ξεῖται, δύο μοῦνοι, τρεῖος ὁ πέμπτος·*
*ὠμὴν ὀπώραν ἢν λάβῃς, οὐ χρήσιμον.*
*Πολλοὺς ἀγῶνας διανύσας λήψη στέφος.*
*Πειρῶ διὰ μέτρου πάντα, μὴ βίᾳ, ποιεῖν.*

If two sixes fall, two ones, the fifth a three:
Gather an unripe fruit, and it is not useful.
After many contests, the laurels will be yours.
But strive with deliberation; do not act in haste
    and violence.

△ △ △ △ △ (bones) — **14444** (coins)

Total Value: 17

Ζεφύρου

Zephyrus

# ZEPHYRUS

*Εἰ δὲ κὲ εἷς χεῖος καὶ τέσσαρα πάντες*
*ἐφεξῆς,*
*νῦν σοὶ πάντα τελεῖ δαίμων καὶ ἐς ὀρθὸν*
*ὁδηγεῖ*
*πράξεις πᾶν κατὰ νοῦν· τῷ μηκέτι τρῦχε*
*σεαυτόν·*
*πάντων ἐντεύξῃ σὺ γ' ἀμέμπτως ὧν*
*ἐπιθυμεῖς.*

If a single one falls, and the rest are fours:
The god will now complete everything for you,
    and guide you favorably.
Act upon all things according to your plans.
    Torment yourself no longer;
You will craft all that you desire with perfection.

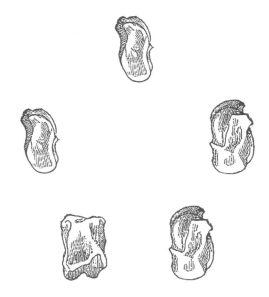

ᗡᗡ△ᗩᗩ (bones) — **66411** (coins)

Total Value: 18

Ἀδραστείας

Adrasteia, She Who None Can Escape

# ADRASTEIA,
## SHE WHO NONE CAN ESCAPE

*Εἰ δὲ δύο ξεῖται, δύο μοῦνοι, τέσσαρ᾽ ὁ*
  *πέμπτος,*
*εὖ πρᾶξιν ταύτην πράξεις καὶ ἐπέσται ὁ*
  *καιρὸς*
*ἐν γενέσει σῴζων καὶ ὁ κίνδυνος παράκειται·*
*καὶ περὶ τῶν ἄλλων μαντειῶν ἐστι καλῶς σοι.*

If two sixes fall, two ones, the fifth a four:
That upon which you act will be positive. Good
    fortune will be yours
from the beginning, and all danger will be swept
    aside.
All other divinations will be positive for you.

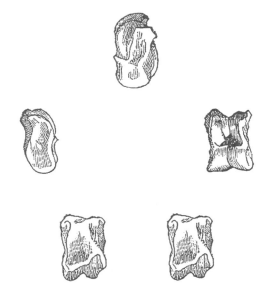

**Λ Ⲥ Δ Δ Γ** (bones) — **16443** (coins)

Total Value: 18

*Διὸς Κεραυνίου*

Zeus the Thunderer

# ZEUS THE THUNDERER

*Εἷς μοῦνος, ξεῖτος, δύο τέσσαρα, τρεῖος ὁ*
  *πέμπτος·*
*οὐκ ἔστιν πράξοντα κατὰ γνώμην ἃ*
  *μεριμνᾷς·*
*οὔτε γὰρ ἐκδήμῳ ἰέναι σοὶ σύνφορόν ἐστιν,*
*οὔτ᾽ ὠνούμενος αἰσθήσῃ ὃ ὀνήσιμον ἔσται.*

A single one, one six, two fours, the fifth a three:
It is not possible to fulfill your desires, the god
  judges;
Nor will it benefit you to journey far from your
  home.
Nor through payment will you find anything
  beneficial.

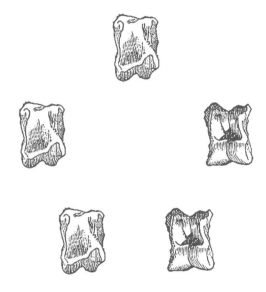

**Δ Δ Δ Γ Γ** (bones) — **44433** (coins)

Total Value: 18

*Δαίμονος Ἱκεσίου*

The Supplicant Deity

# THE SUPPLICANT DEITY

*Πείπτοντες καὶ τετρῶσι τρεῖς καὶ δύο τρῖοι.*
*Οὖ σοι ὁρῶ βουλὴν τήνδε ἀσφαλῆ, ἀλλ'*
*   ἀνάμεινον·*
*εὖ πράξεις, ἔσται σὲ τυχεῖν μετὰ ταῦτα· τὸ*
*   νῦν δὲ*
*ἥσυχος ἦσο, θεοὶς πείθου καὶ ἐπ' ἐλπίδος ἴσθι.*

Three fours, and two threes fall:
I see no safe path for you. Be patient.
Events will favor you after this, but for the present
     do nothing.
Have faith in the gods, and remain hopeful.

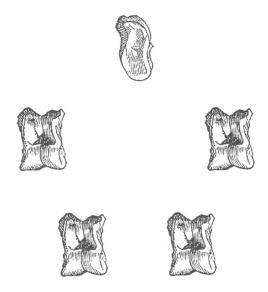

Γ Γ Γ Γ Γ (bones) — 63333 (coins)

Total Value: 18

Ἀγαθοῦ Χρόνου

Benevolent Time

# BENEVOLENT TIME

*Ξείτης, τέσσαρες ὄντες ὁμοῦ τρεία, χρησμὸς*
    *ὅδ᾽ αὐδᾷ·*
*μὴ σπεύσῃς· δαίμων γὰρ ἐνίσταται, ἀλλ᾽*
    *ἀνάμεινον·*
*μηδ᾽ ὥς τὶς τε λέων τυφλὴν ἐκύησε λοχείην·*
*ἥσυχα βουλεύου, καὶ σοὶ χαρίεντα τελεῖται.*

One six, four threes, the following command:
Be in no hurry to move forth; the god disagrees, be
    patient.
Be not like the lioness that bore a den of blind cubs.
Prepare yourself calmly, and all will be happily
    completed in your favor.

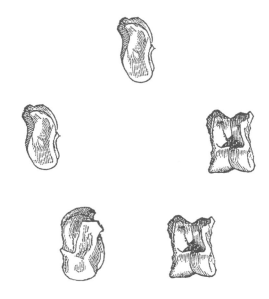

ⱃⱃⱶⱹⱹ (bones) — **66133** (coins)

Total Value: 19

Ἐλπίδος Ἀγαθῆς

Good Hope

# GOOD HOPE

Ἐξεῖται δύο καὶ τρεῖοι, εἷς χεῖος, τάδε
  φράζει·
εὔοδὰ σοι πάντ᾽ ἐστί καὶ ἀσφαλῆ ὧν μ᾽
  ἐπερωτᾷς·
μηδὲ φοβοῦ· δαίμων γὰρ ὁδηγήσει πρὸς
  ἄπαντα,
παύσει ἄφαρ λύπης χαλεπῆς, λύσει δ᾽
  ὑπόνοιαν.

Two sixes and two threes, a single one, so command:
Easily traveled and secure will be your path,
  concerning that which you ask.
Fear nothing; the god will guide you in all things.
He will end the burden of sadness and dissipate
  suspicion.

**Δ Δ Δ Ϲ Δ** (bones) — **44461** (coins)

Total Value: 19

*Διὸς Κτησίου*

Zeus the Creator

# ZEUS THE CREATOR

*Τέσσαρα τρεῖς καὶ ξείτης εἷς καὶ μοῦνος ὁ*
*   πέμπτος·*
*θαρσῶν ἐνχείρει καὶ ἐπ' ἐλπίδος ἐστὶν ὁ*
*   χρησμός,*
*ὃς καταμανύει καὶ τὸν νοσέοντα σεσῶσθαι·*
*εἰ δὲ τί μαντεύῃ χρέος, ὅ χρήσεις ἀπολήμψῃ.*

Three fours, one six, the fifth a one:
Endeavor with courage, for the divination brings you
   hope;
The god declares that he who is ailing will be saved.
And if events impose on you a duty, fulfill it, for you
   will be rewarded.

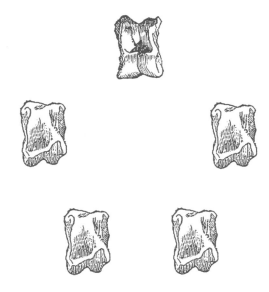

Γ Δ Δ Δ Δ (bones) — 34444 (coins)

Total Value: 19

Ἑρμοῦ Κερδενπόρου

Hermes, Who Presides Over Gain

# HERMES, WHO PRESIDES OVER GAIN

*Εἰ δὲ κὲν εἷς τρεῖος καὶ πάντες τέσσαρα*
  *ἄλλοι,*
*Ἑρμῆς βουλὴν σαῖσι φρεσὶν γὲ καλῶς*
  *ἐπιδρώσει*
*ὠφελίμων ἔνεκ', ἔσται πάντα, ἐπιτεύξῃ ἃ*
  *βούλει·*
*εὑρήσεις δ' ὅσα μαντεύῃ καὶ οὐθὲν κακὸν*
  *ἔσται.*

Should a single three fall, and all the rest fours:
Hermes will grant you the appropriate inspiration;
  he will confer on you a boon.
You will have it all; you will achieve what you desire.
You will discover that which he foretells, and there
  will be no evil.

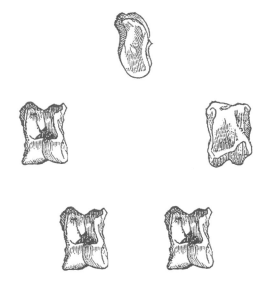

**ΓΓΓΓΔ** (bones) — **63334** (coins)

Total Value: 19

Νείκης Τροπαιοφόρου

Victory Triumphant*

---

*Literally, "Victory Wearing Trophies."

# VICTORY TRIUMPHANT

*Εἷς ξείτης καὶ τρεῖς τρεῖοι καὶ τέσσαρ' ὁ*
*   πέμπτος·*
*μαντείαν ἀγαθὴν ὁρῶ, ξένε, τήνδε νουθεσίαν,*
*καὶ ὃς ἐν ἄλλῃ χώρᾳ ὁδοιπορεῖ, ὁδοῦ λήξειν·*
*σὺν Ζηνὶ μεγίστω τεύξῃ ἐφ ἣν ὁρμᾶς, ἑτοίμως.*

One six and three threes, the fifth a four:
I foresee good things, stranger, in this consultation.
And he who walks in foreign lands will end his
   journey well.
With the help of great Zeus, you will soon achieve
   what you strive for.

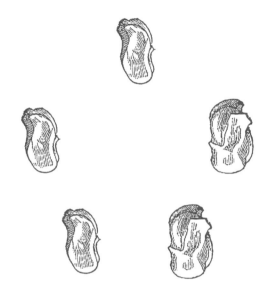

**⊏⊏⊏ΛΛ** (bones) — **66611** (coins)

Total Value: 20

Ἡλίου Νεικηφόρου

The Victorious Sun

# THE VICTORIOUS SUN

*Εἰ δὲ κὲ τρεῖς οἱ ξεῖται, χεῖοι οἱ λοιποί,*
*ἥλιος ὁρᾷ σὲ λαμπρός, ὃς τὰ πάντα ὁρᾷ,*
*τῶν νῦν παρουσῶν συνφορῶν ἕξις λύσιν·*
*νεικηφόρον δώρημα τὸν χρησμὸν τελεῖ.*

If three sixes fall, the rest are ones,
A bright sun watches over you, who sees all things.
For the problems you now face, you will find a
    solution.
A gift that brings victory will complete this
    foretelling.

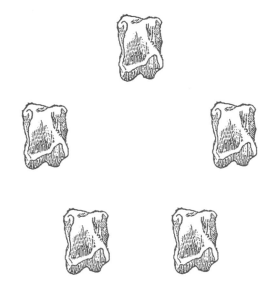

△ △ △ △ △ (bones) — 44444 (coins)

Total Value: 20

Μοιρῶν Οὐρανίων

The Heavenly Fates

# THE HEAVENLY FATES

*Εἰ δὲ κὲ τέσσαρα πάντες ὁμοῦ πείπτωσιν*
  *ὁμοίως,*
*τὸ νῦν ἥσυχος ἧσο, οὐδὲν δ' ὁδὸν νόμισμα*
*αἰσχρὸν γὰρ σοὶ κῆδος ὁρῶ περὶ ὧν μ'*
  *ἐπερωτᾷς·*
*μηδὲ βιάζου θνητὸς ἐών, θεὸν εὐχὴν*
  *ἀποδόσθαι.*

If all the tosses are fours, take no action now;
There is no reward along this path.
For I see guile in you regarding that which you ask
    of me;
Nor should you, a mortal man, pressure the god
    into giving you his blessing.

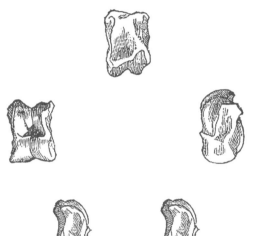

**ΔΓⅭⅭΔ** (bones) — **43661** (coins)

Total Value: 20

Νεμέσεως

Nemesis

# NEMESIS

*Τετρῶος, τρεῖος, ξεῖται δύο, χεῖος ὁ πέμπτος·*
*πρᾶξιν ἐφ ἣν μέλλεις, σπεῦδε· πάντα ἐστί σοι*
 *ἔξω·*
*εἷς ἀγαθὸν τ' ἐν νούσῳ ἐόντα ἥξειν θεὸς*
 *αὐδᾷ·*
*ἥσυχα βουλεύου φρεσίν· ἔσται σοὶ κακὸν*
 *οὐθέν.*

A four, a three, two sixes, the fifth a one:
Concerning that which you intend, make haste; all
  will be yours afterward.
Those things that until now brought you sorrow,
  will be directed to your advantage,
says the god. Be at peace; there is no evil ahead for
  you.

# ⊏ΓΓΔΔ (bones) — 63344 (coins)

## Total Value: 20

Διὸς νεκρῶν κηδεμόνος

## Zeus, The Guardian of the Dead

# ZEUS, THE GUARDIAN OF THE DEAD

*Μοῦνος δ' ἐξείτης, τρεῖοι δύο τέσσαρα δοιά·*
*οὐκ ἔστιν σπεύδοντα τυχεῖν ὅσα καιρὸς*
  *ἀνώγει·*
*κέρδος ἔχεις· πάσης λύσει θεὸς ἐκ κακότητος·*
*εὔκολος ἡ πρᾶξις, μοχθηρὰ δὲ πάντα*
  *φύλαξαι.*

A single six, two threes, and two fours fall:
It is not possible to achieve in haste that which your
  fortune commands.
You will find benefit; the god will relieve you of your
  burden.
The task will be easy, but protect yourself from evil.

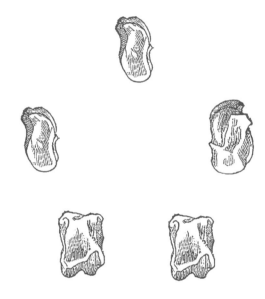

**⊏⊏◬◬◭** (bones) — **66441** (coins)

Total Value: 21

*Δήμητρος*

Demeter

# DEMETER

*Δισσοὶ δ' ἐξεῖται, δύο τέσσαρα, πέμπτος ὁ*
  *χεῖος·*
*εὔοδά σοι παντ' ἐστὶ καὶ ἀσφαλῆ ὧν μ'*
  *ἐπερωτᾷς·*
*μηδὲ φοβοῦ· δαίμων γὰρ ὁδηγήσει πρὸς*
  *ἄπαντα·*
*παύσει γὰρ λύπης χαλεπῆς, λύσει δ'*
  *ὑπόνοιαν.*

Two sixes, two fours, the fifth a one:
Your road will be easy, and all things secure,
    concerning that which you ask.
Fear nothing; the goddess will guide you in all
    things.
She will drive away the burden of sorrow, and
    dissipate suspicion.

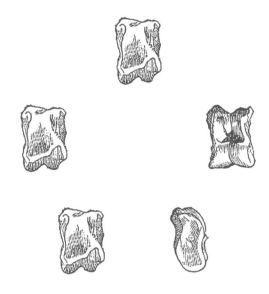

**Δ Δ Δ Ⴀ Γ** (bones) — **44463** (coins)

Total Value: 21

Ἡλίου Φωσφόρου

The Shining Sun

# THE SHINING SUN

*Τέσσαρα τρεῖς, μοῦνος ξείτης καὶ τρεῖος ὁ*
    *πέμπτος·*
*ὅσσα θέλεις πράξεις, εὑρήσεις ὅσσα*
    *μεριμνᾷς·*
*ἐνχείρει, ξένε, θαρσήσας· πάντ' ἐστὶν ἕτοιμα·*
*τἀφανὲς εὑρήσεις, σωτήριον ἦμαρ ἀπαντᾷ.*

Three fours, one six, the fifth a three:
You will achieve what you desire, and will uncover
    that which troubles you.
Endeavor, stranger, with courage, for all is in
    readiness.
You will uncover the hidden; your day of deliverance
    is at hand.

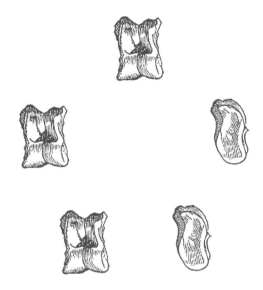

**ΓΓΓⅭⅭ** (bones) — **33366** (coins)

Total Value: 21

*Τύχης εἰς ἄλα προβιβαζούσης*

Good Fortune, Who Delivers Us from Pain

# GOOD FORTUNE,
# WHO DELIVERS US FROM PAIN

*Τρεῖς τρία πείπτοντες, δύο δ᾽ ἐξεῖται, τάδε*
   *φράζει·*
*εἰσὶ καλαὶ πράξεις· σπεύδειν δὲ σὲ χρησμὸς*
   *ὅδ᾽ αὐδᾷ·*
*ἐκφεύξῃ νούσου χαλεπῆς πάντων τὲ*
   *κρατήσεις,*
*καὶ τὸν ἀλώμενον ἐν ξενίῃ ἥξειν θεὸς αὐδᾷ.*

If three threes fall, and two sixes, this they
   command:
There are good deeds; make haste to perform them.
You will be delivered from heavy sorrow and triumph
   over all.
And he who wanders in foreign lands will return
   home, the god declares.

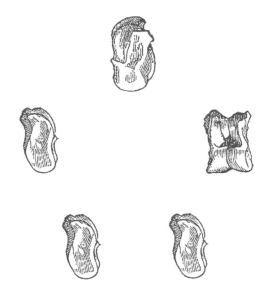

**Λ ⊂⊂⊂Γ** (bones) — **16663** (coins)

Total Value: 22

Μοιρῶν Ἐπιφανῶν

The Renowned Fates

# THE RENOWNED FATES

*Εἷς χεῖος, τρεῖς δ' ἐξεῖται, πέμπτος τρία*
*πείπτων·*
*εἰς στόμα μὴ δῶς χεῖρα λύκῳ, μὴ σοὶ τί*
*γένηται·*
*δυσχερὲς ἐστιν πρᾶγμ' ὑπὲρ οὗ πεύθη καὶ*
*ἄπιστον,*
*ἀλλὰ μέν ἡσύχιος λήξας ὁδοῦ ἠδ' ἀγορασμοῦ.*

A single one, three sixes, the fifth a three:
Put not your hand into the mouths of wolves, for
     you may suffer harm.
What you ask of me is difficult and uncertain.
Even so, you will end this road of unproductive
     wandering in peace.

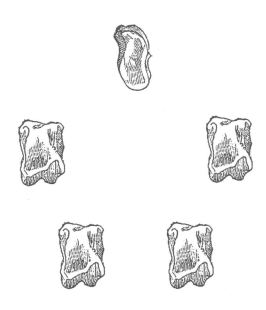

**⊏ △ △ △ △** (bones) — **64444** (coins)

Total Value: 22

*Ποσειδῶνος*

**Poseidon**

# POSEIDON

Ἐξείτης πρῶτος καὶ τέσσαρα πάντες ἐφεξῆς·
εἰς πέλαγος μὴ σπέρμα βαλεῖν καὶ γράμματα
  γράψαι,
ἀμφότερον μόχθος τὲ κενὸς καὶ πρᾶξις
  ἄπρακτος·
μηδὲ βιάζου θνητὸς ἐών θεόν, ὃς σὲ τί βλάψει.

A single six falls, the rest are fours:
Sow not into the sea, nor try to write on the crests of
  waves;
Both are a waste of effort, and an impossible task.
Nor should you, mortal man, make demands of the
  god, who may bring you grief.

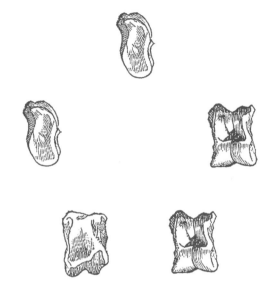

**ⵎⵎΔΓΓ** (bones) — **66433** (coins)

Total Value: 22

Ἄρεως Θουρίου

Raging Ares

# RAGING ARES

*Εἰ δὲ δύο ἐξεῖται εἷς τέσσαρα καὶ δύο τρεῖοι,*
*μὴ βαῖν ἢν βαίνειν μέλλεις, ξένε· τήνδε γὰρ*
*    αὐδῶ·*
*αἴθων ἐσχώρησε λέων μέγας, ὃν πεφύλαξο,*
*δεινός· ἄπρακτος ὁ χρησμός, ἐν ἡσυχίῃ δ᾽*
*    ἀνάμεινον.*

Should two sixes fall, one four, and two threes:
Do not advance toward your goals, stranger. This
    I prophesy:
Into the battle has come a powerful lion; guard
    yourself, for it is terrible.
It is not possible to achieve that which you seek;
    do nothing.

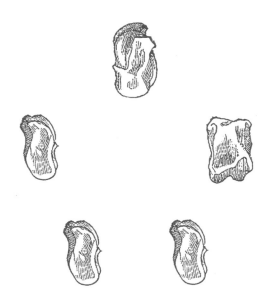

**Λ Ⲉ Ⲉ Ⲉ Δ** (bones) — **16664** (coins)

Total Value: 23

Ἀθηνᾶς

Athena

# ATHENA

*Εἶς χεῖος, τρεῖς δ' ἐξεῖται, καὶ τέσσαρ' ὁ*
*    πέμπτος.*
*Παλλάδ' Ἀθηναίην τείμα, καὶ πάντα σοὶ*
*    ἔσται,*
*ὅσσα θέλεις, καὶ σοὶ τὰ δεδογμένα πάντα*
*    τελεῖται·*
*λύσει δ' ἐκ δεσμῶν καὶ τὸν νοσέοντ'*
*    ἀνασώσει.*

A single one, three sixes, the fifth a four:
Honor Pallas Athena and all will be yours;
All that you desire, and all that you have planned
    for, will come to you.
She will free you from bondage and relieve the ailing
    from pain.

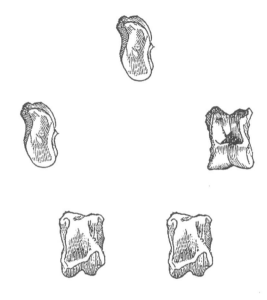

**ⵎⵎ∆∆Γ** (bones) — **66443** (coins)

Total Value: 23

Εὐφροσύνης

Euphrosyne

# EUPHROSYNE

*Εἰ δὲ δύ᾽ ἐξεῖται, δύο τέσσαρα, τρεῖος ὁ*
  *πέμπτος,*
*στέλλε, ὅπου θυμός, σπεύδων, πάλι γὰρ δόμον*
  *ἥξεις·*
*εὑρών καὶ πράξας κατὰ νοῦν πάντων τὲ*
  *κρατήσεις·*
*εὐφροσύνη γὰρ ἄπαντ᾽ ἔσται, σὺ δὲ μήτι*
  *φοβηθῆς.*

Should two sixes fall, two fours, the fifth a three:
Sally forth, follow your instincts, and quickly, for
  you will return home.
Discover what inspires you and act upon it, for you
  will conquer all.
All about you is happiness, and you have nothing to
  fear.

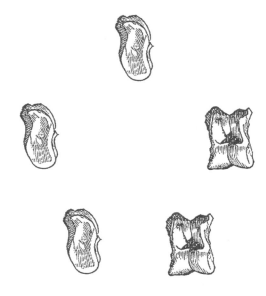

**ⅭⅭⅭΓΓ** (bones) — **66633** (coins)

Total Value: 24

Ἀπόλλωνος Πυθίου

Pythian Apollo

# PYTHIAN APOLLO

*Τρεῖς ὁμοὺ ἐξεῖται, δύο τρεῖοι, μάνθαν'
    ἀκουάν·
μεῖνον, μὴ πράξῃς, Φοίβου χρησμοῖσι δὲ
    πείθου·
ἐν χρόνῳ εὖ καιρὸν τήρει· νῦν δ' ἥσυχος ἴσθι·
μεικρὸν ἐπισχών γὰρ τελέσεις πάνθ' ὅσσα
    μεριμνᾷς.*

Three sixes, and two threes, hear the following:
Stay, do not act, obey the words of the Radiant One.
In the future, lie in wait for your chance, but do
    nothing now.
There are obstacles ahead, but you will complete that
    which concerns you.

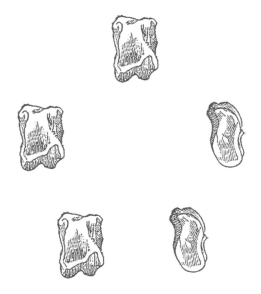

## ∆ ∆ ∆ ⊏ ⊏ (bones) — 44466 (coins)

### Total Value: 24

*Κρόνου Τεχνοφάγου*

## Cronus, Who Devours His Children

# CRONUS, WHO DEVOURS
# HIS CHILDREN

*Τέσσαρα τρεῖς, δύο δ' ἐξεῖται, τάδε σοὶ θεὸς*
  *αὐδᾷ·*
*μίμνε δόμων ἐπὶ σῶν ἀτρέμας μηδ' ἄλλοθι*
  *βαῖνε,*
*μὴ σοι θὴρ ὁλοὸς καὶ ἀλάστωρ ἐγγύθεν ἔλθῃ·*
*οὐ γὰρ ὁρῶ πρᾶξιν τήνδ' ἀσφαλῆ οὐδὲ*
  *βέβαιον.*

Three fours, two sixes, this the god commands:
Remain in your home with serenity; go nowhere else,
lest a fearful and vengeful beast spring out of the
  earth and come against you.
This action appears neither safe nor secure to me.

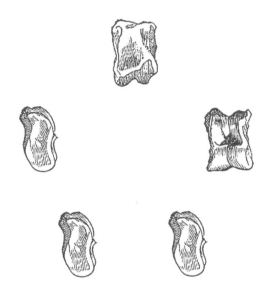

**Δ ⊏ ⊏ ⊏Γ** (bones) — **46663** (coins)

Total Value: 25

*Μηνὸς Φωσφόρου*

The Shining Month

# THE SHINING MONTH

*Τέσσαρα πείπτων εἶς, τρεῖς δ᾽ ἐξεῖται, τρὶ ὁ*
*πέμπτος·*
*θάρσει, καιρὸν ἔχεις, πράξεις δ᾽ ἃ θέλεις,*
*ἐπιτεύξη*
*εἲς ὁδὸν ὁρμηθῆναι· ἔχει καρπὸν τιν᾽ ὁ*
*μόχθος·*
*ἔργον δ᾽ ἐνχειρεῖν ἀγαθὸν καὶ ἀγῶνα δίκην*
*τέ.*

One four falls, three sixes, the fifth a three:
With courage, you will have the opportunity to
    achieve your desire.
You will succeed by dashing to your goal. Your
    efforts will be rewarded.
You are bound, however, to strive for the greater
    good, in a just struggle.

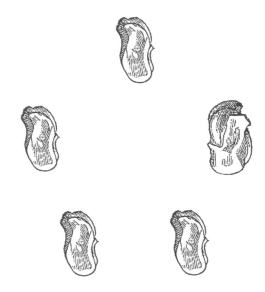

**ⅭⅭⅭⅭⱯ** (bones) — **66661** (coins)

Total Value: 25

Μητρὸς θεῶν

The Mother of the Gods

# THE MOTHER OF THE GODS

*Τέσσαρες ἐξεῖται, πέμπτος χεῖος, τάδε*
  *φράζει·*
*ὡς ἄρνας κατέχουσι λύκοι κρατεροὶ τὲ*
  *λέοντες*
*βοῦς ἕλικας, πάντων οὕτως ἔτι καὶ σὺ*
  *κρατήσεις,*
*καὶ πάντ' ἔσται σοὶ ὅσ' ἐρωτᾷς σὺν Διὸς*
  *Ἑρμῇ.*

Four sixes, the fifth a one, so command:
As wolves snatch sheep, and powerful lions
    seize horned oxen, so will you conquer over all.
All that you ask of me will be yours, with the aid of
    Hermes, son of Zeus.

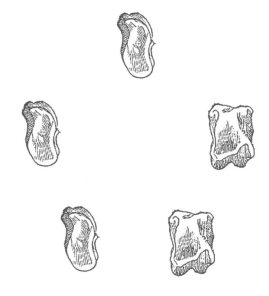

**ᒪᒪᒪ◬◭** (bones) — **66644** (coins)

Total Value: 26

Διὸς Καταχθονίου

Zeus of the Underworld

# ZEUS OF THE UNDERWORLD

*Τρεῖς ὁμοὺ ἐξεῖται, δύο τέσσαρα, χρησμὸς ὅδ᾽*
  *αὐδᾷ·*
*ἡ πρᾶξις κωλύματ᾽ ἔχει, μὴ σπεῦδ᾽,*
  *ἀνάμεινον·*
*λυπηρὰ τὶς ὁδὸς καὶ ἀμήχανος οὐδὲ*
  *προσικτή·*
*ὠνεῖσθαι χαλεπὸν καὶ πωλεῖν τί βλάβος*
  *ἔσται.*

Three sixes, two fours, so do I prophesy:
This act will find barriers ahead; be in no hurry,
  have patience.
For this road bears sadness; it is both inapproachable
  and difficult to traverse.
It will be difficult to buy, and should you sell, it will
  be at a loss.

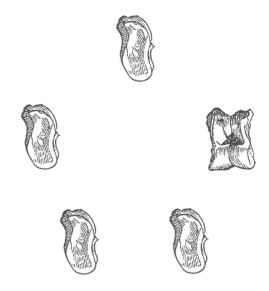

**ⱃ ⱃ ⱃ ⱃ Γ** (bones) — **66663** (coins)

Total Value: 27

*Ἀφροδείτης Οὐρανίας*

Celestial Aphrodite

# CELESTIAL APHRODITE

*Τέσσαρες ἐξεῖται, μοῦνος τρία σοὶ τάδε*
  *φράζει·*
*οὐρανόπαις Ἀφροδείτη, Ἐρώτων πότνι'*
  *ἄνασσα*
*πέμψει μαντείαν ἀγαθήν, δώσει δὲ ὁδὸν σοὶ*
*ἔκφευξίν τε νόσου καὶ φροντίδος*
  *ἀλγεσιθύμου.*

Four sixes and one three command the following:
The daughter of Heaven, Aphrodite, Queen of Love,
will send you good tidings. She will prepare a path
    of escape for you
from the pain and anxiety crushing your heart.

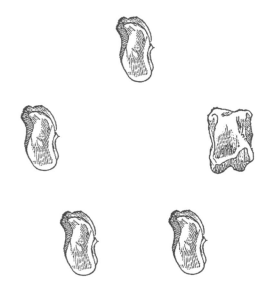

**⊏ ⊏ ⊏ ⊏ ◸** (bones) — **66664** (coins)

Total Value: 28

Βλάβης

Damage

# DAMAGE

*Τέσσαρες ἐξεῖται καὶ τετρῶος τάδε φράζει·*
*οὐκ ἔστιν πρᾶξις· τί μάτην σπεύδεις;*
  *Ἀνάμεινον,*
*μὴ σοὶ σπεύδοντι βλάβος ἐξ αὐτῆς τί γένηται·*
*οὔτε γὰρ εἰς ὁδὸν ὁρμᾶσθαι καλὸν οὔτ᾽*
  *ἀγοράζειν.*

Four sixes and one four command the following:
You will have no luck. Why fight a futile battle?
Stay, for you may be injured in your haste.
It is neither wise to rush toward your goal, nor to
  wander like a fool.

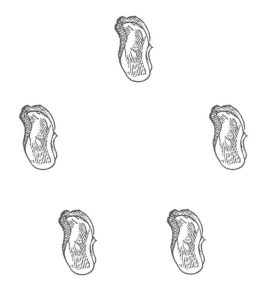

ᴄ ᴄ ᴄ ᴄ ᴄ (bones) — **66666** (coins)

Total Value: 30

Ἑρμοῦ Τετραγώνου

Hermes of the Square

# HERMES OF THE SQUARE

*Εἰ δὲ κὲν ἐξεῖται πάντες πείπτωσιν ὁμοῖοι,*
*μὴ βαῖν᾽ ἢν μέλλεις, μείναντι σοὶ ἔσται*
  *ἄμεινον·*
*αἰσχρὸν γὰρ σοὶ κῆδος ὁρῶ περὶ ὧν μ᾽*
  *ἐπερωτᾷς,*
*ἀλλὰ μέν᾽ ἡσύχιος λήξας ὁδοῦ ἠδ᾽ ἀγορασμοῦ.*

Should all throws be sixes:

Travel not toward your goal; better to stay in place.

For I see guile in you regarding that which you ask
  of me.

Nevertheless, you will end your futile journey in
  peace.

# BIBLIOGRAPHY

Aristotle. *Parts of Animals, Movement of Animals, Progression of Animals.* Translated by A. L. Peck and E. S. Forster. Cambridge, Mass.: Loeb Classical Library, 1937.

Arundell, Reverand F. V. J. *Discoveries in Asia Minor, Including a Description of the Ruins of Several Ancient Cities.* Vol. 2. London: R. Bentley, 1834.

Aurelius, Marcus. *The Meditations.* Edited by Paul Halsall. New York: Fordham University History Department, Internet Ancient History Sourcebook, 1998. www.fordham.edu/halsall/ancient/marcuaurelius1. asp (accessed June 21, 2013).

Cousin, G. *Bulletin de Correspondance Hellènique.* S. 496*ff.* 1884.

Gilmour, G. H. "The Nature and Function of Astragalus Bones from Archaeological Contexts in the Levant and Eastern Mediterranean." *Oxford Journal of Archaeology* 16, no. 2 (July 1997): 167.

Heinevetter, F. *Würfel- und Buchstabenorakel in Griechenland und Kleinasien.* Inaugural Dissertation. Breslau, Germany: Grasz, Barth, and Co., 1912.

Hirschfeld, G. *Monatsberichte der Berliner Akademie.* 1875: 167.

Homer. *The Iliad.* Translated by Samuel Butler. Cambridge, Mass.: MIT, The Internet Classics Archive, 1994. http://classics.mit.edu/Homer/ iliad.html (accessed June 24, 2013).

*Journal of Hellenic Studies* 8 (1887).

Kaibel, G. "Ein Würfelorakel." *Hermes* 10 (1876).

———. *Epigrammata Graeca ex Lapidibus Conlecta.* Berlin, 1878.

———. "Inschriften aus Pisidien." *Hermes* 23 (1888).

Lanckoroński, K. *Die Städte Pamphyliens und Pisidiens.* Vol. 2. Vienna, Austria, 1892.

Petersen, E. v. Luschan, F. *Reisen in südwestlichen Kleinasien.* Vol. 2, *Reisen in Lykien, Milyas und Kibyratis.* Vienna, Austria, 1889.

Plato. *Philebus.* http://classics.mit.edu/Plato/philebus.html (accessed June 21, 2013).

Proclus. *On the Theology of Plato.* Charleston, S.C.: Nabu Press, 2012.

Sterrett, J. R. Sitlington. "An Epigraphical Journey in Asia Minor." *Papers of the American School of Classical Studies at Athens* 2, nos. 56–58 (1883–1884).

# LIST OF DIVINATION
# COMBINATIONS

Consult the table on page 13 to determine the value of each coin toss. The order of the five numerical values of your coin tosses does not matter. For example, 11113 and 11311 are considered the same combination— you would consult the same divination for both variations.

| Total Value | Coin Toss Value Combinations | Page Number |
|---|---|---|
| Five | 11111 | 48 |
| Seven | 11113 | 50 |
| Eight | 11114 | 52 |
| Nine | 33111 | 54 |
| Ten | 61111 | 56 |
| Ten | 11143 | 58 |
| Eleven | 33311 | 60 |
| Eleven | 11144 | 62 |
| Twelve | 11136 | 64 |
| Twelve | 11334 | 66 |
| Thirteen | 11164 | 68 |
| Thirteen | 11344 | 70 |
| Thirteen | 33331 | 72 |

| Total Value | Coin Toss Value Combinations | Page Number |
|---|---|---|
| Fourteen | 13334 | 74 |
| Fourteen | 61133 | 76 |
| Fourteen | 44411 | 78 |
| Fifteen | 13344 | 80 |
| Fifteen | 11166 | 82 |
| Fifteen | 33333 | 84 |
| Fifteen | 43611 | 86 |
| Sixteen | 63331 | 88 |
| Sixteen | 64411 | 90 |
| Sixteen | 13444 | 92 |
| Sixteen | 33334 | 94 |
| Seventeen | 33344 | 96 |
| Seventeen | 13346 | 98 |
| Seventeen | 11366 | 100 |
| Seventeen | 14444 | 102 |
| Eighteen | 66411 | 104 |
| Eighteen | 16443 | 106 |
| Eighteen | 44433 | 108 |
| Eighteen | 63333 | 110 |
| Nineteen | 66133 | 112 |
| Nineteen | 44461 | 114 |
| Nineteen | 34444 | 116 |
| Nineteen | 63334 | 118 |
| Twenty | 66611 | 120 |
| Twenty | 44444 | 122 |
| Twenty | 43661 | 124 |
| Twenty | 63344 | 126 |
| Twenty-one | 66441 | 128 |
| Twenty-one | 44463 | 130 |
| Twenty-one | 33366 | 132 |

| Total Value | Coin Toss Value Combinations | Page Number |
|---|---|---|
| Twenty-two | 16663 | 134 |
| Twenty-two | 64444 | 136 |
| Twenty-two | 66433 | 138 |
| Twenty-three | 16664 | 140 |
| Twenty-three | 66443 | 142 |
| Twenty-four | 66633 | 144 |
| Twenty-four | 44466 | 146 |
| Twenty-five | 46663 | 148 |
| Twenty-five | 66661 | 150 |
| Twenty-six | 66644 | 152 |
| Twenty-seven | 66663 | 154 |
| Twenty-eight | 66664 | 156 |
| Thirty | 66666 | 158 |

# BOOKS OF RELATED INTEREST

**The Magus of Java**
Teachings of an Authentic Taoist Immortal
*by Kosta Danaos*

**The Complete I Ching — 10th Anniversary Edition**
The Definitive Translation
*by Taoist Master Alfred Huang*

**Oracles of the Dead**
Ancient Techniques for Predicting the Future
*by Robert Temple*

**Gods of the Runes**
The Divine Shapers of Fate
*by Frank Joseph*
*Illustrated by Ian Daniels*

**The Divining Mind**
A Guide to Dowsing and Self-Awareness
*by T. E. Ross and Richard D. Wright*

**Ogam: The Celtic Oracle of the Trees**
Understanding, Casting, and Interpreting the
Ancient Druidic Alphabet
*by Paul Rhys Mountfort*

**How to Read Signs and Omens in Everyday Life**
*by Sarvananda Bluestone, Ph.D.*

**Pendulum Power**
A Mystery You Can See, A Power You Can Feel
*by Greg Nielsen and Joseph Polansky*

INNER TRADITIONS • BEAR & COMPANY
P.O. Box 388
Rochester, VT 05767
1-800-246-8648
www.InnerTraditions.com

Or contact your local bookseller